iPhone 11

The Latest User Manual for Beginners, Kids, Teens, and Seniors

Blikz Phaggi

Copyright © 2019 Blikz Phaggi

All rights reserved. No part of this publication may be reproduced, distributed, or transmitted in any form or by any means, including photocopying, recording, or other electronic or mechanical methods, without the prior written permission of the publisher, except in the case of brief quotations embodied in critical reviews and specific other non-commercial uses permitted by copyright law.

ISBN: 978-1-63750-221-1

Table of Contents

IPHONE 11 1

INTRODUCTION 6

CHAPTER 1 9

    HOW TO SET UP YOUR BRAND-NEW IPHONE 11 9
    SETUP IPHONE 11 THE CORRECT WAY 9
    IPHONE 11 SET UP: THE FUNDAMENTALS 10
    AUTO SETUP FOR IPHONE 11 11
    SET UP A FRESH IPHONE 11 FROM SCRATCH 12
    RESTORING FROM A BACK-UP OF YOUR OLD IPHONE 13
    SET UP FACE ID 13
    CREATE IPHONE EMAIL 15
        Advanced iPhone Email tweaks 16
    MANAGE CALENDARS, ICLOUD, COMMUNICATIONS AND MORE 17
    SECURE YOUR WEB EXPERIENCE 19
    ICLOUD EVERYWHERE 20
    SERVICES SUBSCRIPTION DURING IPHONE SETUP 21
    MORE IPHONE SET UP TWEAKS 22

CHAPTER 2 25

    THE IPHONE 11 AND IPHONE 11 PRO 25
    APPLE DESIGN HEADING A DIFFERENT WAY 26
    THE IPHONE 11 CAMERA 26
    DISPLAY SCREEN TECHNOLOGY 28
    IMPROVING THE CAMERA APP 29
    A13 BIONIC CPU 31
    WHAT WASN'T TOLD ABOUT IPHONE 11 33

CHAPTER 3 34

    IPHONE 11 MOST DESIRED FEATURES 34

CHAPTER 4 42

    HOW TO CUSTOMIZE YOUR IPHONE MOBILE 42

CHAPTER 5 53

IOS 13 UPDATE AND FEATURES 53
THE TWO-MINUTE IOS 13 REVIEW 54
IOS 13.1 UPDATE 58
IOS 13.1 BUG FIXES 59
IOS 13.1 NEW FEATURES 59
  iOS 13 compatibility list 62
  iOS 13 Dark Mode 63
  iOS 13 offers 'FaceTime attention correction' 65
  iOS 13 on iPad is iPadOS, and it's a big change 65
  iOS 13 includes a QuickPath keyboard 67
  iOS 13 debuts new 'Find My' app 68
  iOS 13 makes your old iPhone faster, go longer 68
  Reminders gets a large overhaul 69
  Camera and portrait Mode changes 70
  New Siri tone of voice sounds more natural 71
  Memoji gets make-up, Text messages get info sharing 72

CHAPTER 6 74

HOW TO CREATE & USE IPHONE 11 SHORTCUTS 74

CHAPTER 7 79

RECOMMENDED IPHONE APPLICATIONS 79

CHAPTER 8 96

IPHONE 11 GESTURES YOU SHOULD KNOW 96
USING MEMOJI 99
IOS 13 IPHONE 11 NOTIFICATION TIPS 100
USING SCREEN TIME 101
SIRI SHORTCUTS 103
IPHONE 11 CONTROL CENTRE TIPS 103
IPHONE 11 PHOTOS AND CAMERA TIPS 106
IPHONE 11: KEYBOARD TIPS 109
FACE ID TIPS 110
IPHONE 11: SCREEN TIPS 110
IPHONE 11 BATTERY TIPS 111

CHAPTER 9 114

HOW TO UNLOCK ITS PHOTOGRAPHIC POTENTIAL 114

CHAPTER 10 122

RESTORING iPHONE 11 BACKUP FROM iCLOUD AND iTUNES 122
How to Move Data From an Android Phone *127*
How to Restore iPhone 11 Back-up from iCloud or iTunes *135*

CHAPTER 11 143

HOW TO START DARK MODE ON iPHONE 11 143
WHAT DOES DARK MODE IN iOS 13 DO? 144
HOW TO UPGRADE APPLICATIONS ON YOUR iPHONE IN iOS 13 145
DO APPLICATIONS AUTOMATICALLY UPGRADE IN iOS 13? 146

CHAPTER 12 147

iPHONE 11 TIPS & TRICKS 147

CHAPTER 13 152

HOW TO MAXIMIZE iPHONE 11 152
HOW TO UNLOCK YOUR iPHONE WITH RAISE TO WAKE 154
HOW TO UNLOCK THE iPHONE 11 & NEWER iPHONES 155
HOW TO OPEN UP THE CONTROL & NOTIFICATION CENTRES................. 156
HOW TO GO BACK TO THE HOME SCREEN FROM AN APP 157
HOW TO ACTIVATE APPLE PAY 157
HOW TO POWER OFF THE iPHONE 11 158
HOW TO ACCESS SIRI WITH SIDE BUTTON 159
HOW TO TAKE SCREENSHOTS WITHOUT THE HOME BUTTON 160
HOW TO ENABLE & ACTIVATE REACHABILITY 160
How to Change Between & Force Quit Apps *162*
HOW TO SWITCH OFF POWER & PERFORM A HARD RESTART 163
HOW TO TEMPORARILY DISABLE FACE ID 165

INDEX 167

Introduction

Do you just acquire an iPhone 11 and iPhone 11 Pro or iPhone 11 Pro Max, for the first time, or you probably need in-depth tips and tutorials on how to use your device optimally? This is the guide you need.

The iPhone 11, iPhone 11 Pro, and iPhone 11 Pro Max, which are the latest addition to the Apple invention is finally out after much anticipations and speculations.

With this concise book, you will be guided by hand to the tips, shortcuts, and workarounds that will turn you into an iPhone master in less than 30 minutes of reading this book.

Among what you would learn are;
- iPhone 11 correct set-up process
- iPhone 11 Series Features
- How to personalize your iPhone 11, iPhone 11 pro and iPhone 11 Pro Max
- iPhone 11 Series Security Features
- Apple ID and Face ID

- The top year 2020 iPhone 11 Applications to use
- Reducing the Passcode Activation date
- Apple Face ID Hidden Features
- All iPhone 11 Gestures you should know
- How to Hide SMS notification content display on iPhone screen
- Erasing/Deactivating Keyboard Dictionary
- How to use the virtual Home button
- How to enable limited USB settings
- Best Shortcuts you are never aware of
- Disabling Location-Based iAds
- iPhone 11, iPhone 11 pro and iPhone 11 Pro Max Tips and Tricks

...and a lot more.

There's no better resource around for dummies and seniors like this bestselling guide. It's a must-have manual that every iPhone user must-own and also be gifted to friends and family.

It is the complete guide for you, as you would get simplified follow-through instructions on every possible thing you should know about iPhone 11, iPhone 11 pro and iPhone 11 Pro Max, how you can customize the iPhone as well as amazing Tips & tricks you never would find in the original iPhone manual.

Chapter 1

How to Set up Your brand-new iPhone 11

For many individuals, the iPhone 11 Series would radically not be the same as the previous iPhone model. Not surprisingly, the iPhone set up process hasn't transformed much. However, you might end up on the familiar ground; you may still find a lot of little things you honestly must do before you switch ON your new phone for the very first time (or soon after that).

Let's check out how to set up your brand-new iPhone 11 the proper way.

Setup iPhone 11 the Correct Way

With iPhone 11, you'll have the ability to take benefit of Apple's Automatic Setup. If you're on an updated iPhone without Face Identification, you would see that Touch ID is entirely gone. (Which means you'll save one face, rather than several.)

If you're a serial upgrader, and you're from the year-old

iPhone X, less has changed. But you'll still need to update just as usual.

iPhone 11 Set up: The Fundamentals

Re-download only the applications you would need; that one is crucial. Most of us have so many applications on our iPhones that people do not use; this is the big reason we execute a clean set up, in all honesty. Utilize the App Store application and make sure you're authorised into the Apple accounts. (Touch the tiny icon of the Updates - panel to see which accounts you're logged on to.) Only download applications you've found in the past half a year. Or, be daring: download stuff you Utilize regularly. We're prepared to wager it'll be considered a very few.

Set up **DO NOT Disturb** - If you're like ordinary people, you're constantly getting notifications, iMessages, and other types of distractions through to your iPhone. Create **DO NOT Disturb** in the Configurations application (it's in the next section listed below, slightly below *Notifications* and *Control Centre*). You'll want to routine it for occasions when you need never to be bothered.

Toggle Alarm to On and then Messages when you want to keep Notifications away from that person. Try 9 p.m. to 8 a.m. when you can.

Pro suggestion: *Let some things through if there's an Emergency: Enable Allow Phone calls From your Favourites and toggle Repeated Phone calls to On. iOS 13 also enables you to switch on DO NOT Disturb at Bedtime, which mutes all notifications and even hides them from the lock screen, and that means you don't get distracted when you take the phone to check the time.*

Auto Setup for iPhone 11

Secondly; Auto Setup enables you to duplicate your Apple ID and home Wi-Fi configurations from another device, simply by getting them close collectively.

In case your old iPhone (or iPad) has already been operating iOS 12 or iOS 13, to put it simply the devices next to one another. Then follow the prompts to avoid needing to enter your Apple ID and Wi-Fi passwords;

this makes the original iPhone set up much smoother.

Set up a fresh iPhone 11 from Scratch

The guide below assumes you're establishing your brand-new iPhone from scratch. If you don't wish to accomplish that, you'll need to acquire any of the other iPhone manuals for beginners that I have written.

Restoring from a back-up of Your old iPhone

You'll probably be restoring your brand-new iPhone from a back-up of your present iPhone. If that's so, then you merely want to do a couple of things:

- Be sure you come with an up-to-date backup.

- Use Apple's new Auto Setup feature to get you started.

The first thing is as simple as going to the iCloud configurations on your iPhone, and looking at that, they're surely a recent automated back-up. If not, do one by hand. Head to *Configurations > Your Name > iCloud > iCloud Back-up and tap* **BACKUP Now**. Wait around until it is done.

Set up Face ID

Face ID is much simpler to use than Touch ID, and it's also simpler to create. Instead of needing to touch your iPhone with your fingerprints, one at a time, you simply check out the camera, and that's almost it. To create Face ID on your iPhone, do the next when prompted through the preliminary iPhone setup. (If you'd like to begin over with a phone you set up previously, check out *Settings > Face ID & Passcode, and type in your password, to begin.*)

Establishing Face ID is similar to the compass calibration your iPhone enables you to do from time to time when you use the Maps app. Only rather than rolling the iPhone around, you turn your head. You'll need to do two scans, and then the iPhone 11 would have your 3D head stored in its Secure Enclave, inaccessible to anything, even to iOS itself (despite some clickbait "news" stories).

Now, still, in Settings/*Configurations > Face ID & Passcode*, you can pick which features to use with Face ID, as everyone else did with *Touch ID*.

If you regularly sport another appearance - you're a clown, a doctor, an impersonator, or something similar -

14

then additionally, you should create another impression. Just tap the button in the facial ID settings to set this up.

Create iPhone Email

- *Add your email accounts* - Whether you utilize Mail, Perspective, or something similar to Sparrow, you'll want to include your email accounts immediately. For Apple's Email app, touch *Configurations > Accounts & Passwords, then tap Add Accounts*. Choose your email supplier and follow the steps to enter all the knowledge required.

- *See more email preview* - Email lets you start to see the content of a note without starting it. May as well see as a lot of it as you possibly can, right? Utilize Settings > Email and tap on the Preview button. Change your configurations to five lines and get more information from your email messages and never have to get them open up.

- *Established your default accounts* - For reasons unknown, our iOS Email settings always appear to default to a merchant account we never use, like *iCloud*. Tap *Configurations > Accounts & Passwords > Your email accounts name, and then touch Accounts > Email*. Once you reach the depths of the settings, you can touch your preferred email; this would be your address in new mails. (When there is only one address in here, you're all set.) That is also the spot to add some other email addresses associated with your email account.

Advanced iPhone Email tweaks

- *Swipe to control email* - It's much more helpful to have the ability to swipe your email messages away rather than clicking through and tapping on several control keys. Swipe to Archive, so that whenever you swipe that path, you'll have the ability to either quickly save a contact to your Archive. Or, if your email accounts support swiping left as a default Delete action, it'll offer a Garbage icon. Swipe left to Tag as Read, which is a smart way to slam through your electronic mails as you have them. This only impacts your built-in

Email application from Apple. Each third-party email customer can do things differently.

- *Add an HTML signature* - A sound email signature really can cause you to look professional, so make sure to include an HTML signature to your email. If you've already got one on the desktop, duplicate and paste the code into contact and ahead to yourself.

You'll be able to copy and paste it into an Email application (or whichever email supplier you like, if it facilitates it). It could be as easy as textual content formatting tags or as complicated as adding a logo design from a webserver. You should use an iOS application to make one, too; however, they tend to look fairly basic.

Manage Calendars, iCloud, Communications and more

- *Set default Calendar alert times* - Calendar is ideal for alerting you to important occasions, but it's not necessarily at a convenient or useful time.

Established the default timing on three types of occasions: Birthdays, Occasions, and All-Day Occasions, and that means you get reminders when they're helpful. Utilize *Configurations > Calendars*. Tap on Default Alert Times and set your Birthday reminders to 1 day before, your Occasions to quarter-hour before (or a period which makes more sense to your mind), and All-Day Occasions on the day of the function (10 a.m.). You'll never miss a meeting again.

- ***Background application refresh*** - You'll desire to be selective about which applications you desire to be in a position to run in the background, so have a look at the list in *Settings > General > Background App Refresh*. Toggle Background App Refresh to ON, then toggle OFF all the applications you don't need being able to access anything in the background. When in question, toggle it to OFF and find out if you are slowed up by any applications that require to refresh when you release them. You'll want to allow

Background Refresh for Cult of Macintosh Magazine!

Secure Your Web Experience

- *Browser set up* - Surfing the net is filled with forms to complete. Adding your name, address, email, and bank cards may take up a great deal of your power. Make sure to head into Configurations > Browser > AutoFill to create your mobile internet browser the proper way. First, toggle Use Contact Info to On. Then tap on My Info and select the contact you want to use when you encounter form areas in Browser. Toggle Titles and Passwords on as well, and that means you can save that across appointments to the same website. (This pulls from *iCloud Keychain*, so make sure to have that allowed, too.)

Toggle *CREDIT CARDS* to ON as well, which means you can shop swiftly. (*be sure only to use SSL-encrypted websites.*)

Pro suggestion: Manage which bank cards your iPhone

helps you to save with a tap on BANK CARDS. You can include new cards within, or delete ones that no more work or that you don't want to use via mobile Browser.

The browser in iOS 13 and later version also blocks cross-site monitoring, which are those cookies that follow you around and let online stores place the same advertisements on every subsequent web page you visit. That is On by default, and that means you should not do anything. Just relax and revel in your newfound personal privacy.

iCloud Everywhere

- *iCloud is everything* - There's without a doubt in our thoughts that iCloud is the easiest, optimum solution for keeping all of your stuff supported and safe. Utilize the Configurations > iCloud and be sure to register with your **Apple ID**. You can manage your storage space in here, but make sure to enable all you need immediately. Enable iCloud Drive, Photos, Connections, Reminders, Browser, Records, News, Wallet, Back-up, Keychain and others once you get the iPhone unpacked. You can enable Email and Calendars if you merely use Apple's applications and services; usually, you would keep those toggled OFF.

Services subscription during iPhone setup

- ***Enable iCloud Photo Library*** - We love the iCloud Photo Library. It maintains your photos and videos securely stored in the cloud and enable you to get full-quality copies of your documents in the event you misplace your originals. iCloud Picture Library depends on your iCloud storage space, if you have a lot of photos, you'll want to bump that up. Utilize Configurations > iCloud > Photos, then toggle iCloud Image Library to On. (Remember that this will switch off My Picture Stream. If you'd like both, you'll need to re-toggle Image Stream back again to On.)

- ***Use iTunes Match*** - Sure, Apple Music monitors all the music data files on your devices, but if you delete them from your iPhone and don't have a back-up elsewhere, you're heading to have to stay for whatever quality Apple Music will provide you with when you listen. If you wish to maintain your full-resolution music documents supported to the cloud, use iTunes Match.

You get all of your music files matched up or published to iCloud in the best bitrate possible. After that, you can stream or download the music to any device provided your iTunes Match membership is intact. Never be without your music (or have an over-filled iPhone) again. Go to *Configurations > Music*. Then touch on Sign up to iTunes Match to understand this valuable service allowed on your brand-new iPhone.

More iPhone set up Tweaks

- *Extend your Auto-Lock* - Let's face it. The default two minutes you get for the Volume of time your iPhone would remain on without turning off its screen may keep the battery higher much longer, but it's insufficient for anybody during regular use.

Utilize Configurations, General, Auto-Lock to create this to the whole five minutes, which means you can stop tapping your screen at all times to keep it awake.

- *Get texts everywhere* - You can enable your Mac PC or iPad to get texts from your iPhone, provided you've set up iMessage to them (Settings, Text messages, toggle iMessage to ON on any iOS device, Messages Preferences on your Mac). Ensure that your other device is close by when you Utilize Settings on your iPhone, then touch Messages > TEXT Forwarding. Any devices available will arrive on the list. Toggle your Mac or iPad to On, and then check the prospective device for a code. Enter that code into your iPhone. Now all of your devices are certain to get not only iMessages but also texts from those not using iMessage.

- *Equalise your tunes* - Start the EQ in your Music application to be able to hear your preferred jams and never have trouble with a Bluetooth speaker.

Go to Configurations > Music. Once there, touch on EQ and established your iPhone to NIGHT TIME; this will provide you with a great quantity rise for those times where you want to blast *The Clash* while you make a quick supper in the kitchen.

Chapter 2

The iPhone 11 and iPhone 11 Pro

It took me a defeat to understand the new iPhone 11, in fact, Apple's successor to the iPhone XR rather than the offspring of the high-end iPhone XS; this subtle shift in the merchandise line, which walks from the iPhone "X" model and also repositions the baseline iPhone as a slightly less able device that you can purchase for a considerable number of dollars significantly lesser than Apple's most effective smartphone, maybe Apple's smartest little bit of rebranding.

iPhone 11	iPhone 11 Pro	iPhone 11 Pro Max
6.1-inch LCD	5.8-inch OLED	6.5-inch OLED
1792 x 828 at 326 ppi	2436 x 1125 at 458 ppi	2688 x 1242 at 458 ppi
No 3D Touch	No 3D Touch	No 3D Touch
Face ID	Face ID	Face ID
A13 Chip	A13 Chip	A13 Chip
4GB RAM	6GB RAM	6GB RAM
12MP front camera	12MP front camera	12MP front camera
Dual 12MP rear cameras	Triple 12MP rear cameras	Triple 12MP rear cameras
Bilateral wireless charging	Bilateral wireless charging	Bilateral wireless charging
WiFi 6	WiFi 6	WiFi 6
No Apple Pencil support	Apple Pencil support	Apple Pencil support
Glass design	Frost glass design	Frost glass design
3,110 mAh battery	3,190+ mAh battery	3,500+ mAh battery
64GB/256GB/512GB	128GB/256GB/512GB	128GB/256GB/512GB
Starting at $749	Starting at $999	Starting at $1099

Apple Design Heading a Different Way

Labels aren't as important as the design and features, and no matter which new iPhone 11 you choose-if you select one-Apple, they will provide good video cameras, more electric battery life, better level of resistance to the elements and, of course, they'll all dispatch with iOS 13, that includes a lot of useful mobile operating-system updates.

I noticed lots of people who comment on Twitter weren't kind to the new design on iPhone 11, as they perceived it as a clunky design choice, but they're responding to photos of the device.

The iPhone 11 Camera

I handled all three cell phones, and the camera arrays are distinctive, they don't stick out just as much as you'd think; this is due to the somewhat surprising process Apple uses to produce the iPhone 11 and iPhone 11 Pro back, it is just one piece of cup (a brushed back on the iPhone 11 Pro and shiny on the iPhone 11) that Apple milled down while departing the camera array elevated.

It's the type of design many people will readily make to access Apple's new 120-level field of view ultra-wide 12 MP camera, which is on both models. All iPhone 11 models likewise have a typical wide-angle 12 MP camera. The iPhone 11 Pro provides the 2X optical focus camera.

All of those other design, incidentally, is unchanged. All of the mobile phones still have the notch for the True depth Component, which now includes a 12 MP selfie camera with the capacity of slow-motion video for "selfies.

Display Screen Technology

I doubt if anyone could tell the difference between iPhone 11 and iPhone XR, XS, and XS Max, which includes the same screen technology and quality as the iPhone XR. Apple upgrades the body of all the cell phones, as *iPhone 11 can handle thirty minutes under 2 meters of water, and iPhone 11 Pro can handle thirty minutes under 4 meters of water*; this appears to be that they're ready for a swim.

Just like the iPhone XR, the iPhone 11 gets the majority of the cool colours; however, the metal iPhone 11 Pro is no slouch: It gets a new Midnight-Green option (exquisite). Each one of these devices seems excellent and stable in hands. I especially liked the feel of the iPhone 11 Pro's brushed cup back.

Apple, naturally, pushed the visual envelope on the $999 iPhone 11 Pro, which includes what's called a brilliant Retina *XDR screen* (it's **OLED**), which is a name that needs to be familiar to the people who followed the Mac PC Pro information from earlier this year 2019. I don't know if the eye can visually process *458 PPI*, but I'll say that the images and video (*up to 4K 60 FPS*) on the iPhone 11 Pro were stunning. Also, the audio, which now helps Dolby Atmos, was almost noisy enough to conquer the very occupied demo room.

Improving the Camera App

Consumers might be most thinking about the amount of

change apple has infiltrated in camera and video applications to aid all the new *iPhone 11, iPhone 11 pro* and *iPhone 11 Pro* max photographic features. Rather than hard switches between lens, Apple redesigned the native apps to aid smooth transitions with swipes and arc scrolls.

Apple's Phil Schiller before the projected image of a three-camera selection of iPhone 11 Pro

To place a more exceptional point on the Camera Apps requires continuous knowledge on all the lenses, the standard picture window concurrently shows the ultra-wide image in the greyed-out areas on either part of the picture.

You can view instantly how an ultra-wide shot might look; furthermore, the indigenous video app is now able to do some aesthetic video edits, controlling brightness, comparison, and even permitting you to crop your video (sometimes you won't realize how much you skipped it until you begin cropping randomly out of your video backgrounds).

Several picture features represent Apple getting up to its competitors, but at least Apple always manages to place its spin on the updates. Regarding *Night Mode Setting*, Apple has finally made the feature automated, which is smart because most consumers don't want to take into account photo changing configurations. The test images I noticed appeared amazing.

A13 Bionic CPU

Apple's new ***A13 Bionic CPU*** has *8.5 billion processors*, which it uses to do some pretty impressive image-processing gymnastics; it can help the iPhone 11 execute a trillion procedures on each image, but I have been intrigued with what Apple says is arriving later, which is called *"Deep Fusion,"* this is a leading-edge. *Neural Engine-backed* procedure somehow requires nine photos before you even press the shutter, the engine then creates one properly uncovered and detail-rich picture out of everything. It seems crazy, and I'm just a little unfortunate that we'll have to hold back for Apple to include it to the *iPhone 11 Pro*.

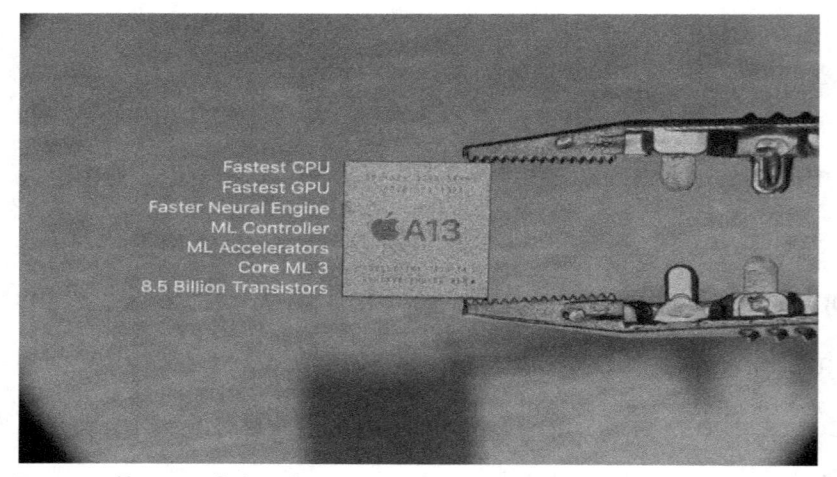

Regardless of the increased power, Apple claims that the iPhone 11 Pro gets 4 hours more battery life than the iPhone XS Max. I usually take these electric battery performance statements with a grain of sodium. However, battery life mainly depends on what you're doing with the phone.

What wasn't told about iPhone 11

Oddly, there is no reference to new wireless charging features. Everyone expected Apple to unveil something such as *Samsung's cellular PowerShare*, which would've to allow iPhone share power, wirelessly charging AirPod 2 devices. Apple also mentioned improved Face Identification Speed multiple times while preventing the apparent fingerprint. It appears that Apple may soon be the only major smartphone producer who's not concealing biometric security.

Finally, there is not a single reference to 5G technology; 5G would strike NEW YORK and other major urban centres throughout the year 2020. Apple made a technique that required the ultra-popular XR and improved it with another camera and the latest CPU while keeping the purchase price at $699, and it forced the envelope on the iPhone 11 Pro Max.

Chapter 3

iPhone 11 most Desired Features

1. *Six New Gorgeous Colours*

The brand new iPhone 11 would come in six beautiful new colours; they're a little more in the pastel-colour range; however, they look quite right. The colours are *Crimson, White, Green, Yellowish, Dark, and Red.*

2. *Anodised Aluminium and 3D Cup Design*

As you can tell by looking at the back, the iPhone 11 has a fresh design at the end. The iPhone 11 shell is manufactured out of anodized aluminum, and on both edges, there's glass -panel. iPhone 11 includes a 3D cup design that seamlessly merges with the lightweight aluminum band.

3. *A13 Bionic Chip*

Apple says that the 7mm+ based *A13 Bionic chip* gets the fastest CPU in virtually any smartphone. It is up to 20% faster than the CPU inside the A12 chip. The A13 chip has special improvements for machine learning accelerators that permit the CPU to provide more than 1 trillion procedures per second.

4. *Fastest Smartphone GPU in the World*

Apple also says that the iPhone 11 gets the quickest GPU in virtually any smartphone in the marketplace. It's up to 20% faster than the GPU in iPhone XR while also being more power-efficient.

5. *New Main Camera*

The primary camera on the iPhone 11 has been updated; the 12MP sensor has 100% Concentrate Pixels for three times faster autofocus in low light.

6. *New Ultra Wide Camera*

The iPhone 11 gets an entirely new camera, and it's an ultra-wide sensor with a 120-level wide field of view; the 12MP Ultra Wide sensor has an f/2.4 aperture. It gives you to zoom out by 0.5x from the standard shot. By using this camera, you may take some fantastic cinematic shots with an entirely new perspective.

7. *4K Video on Ultra-Wide Camera*

The 4K recording works on the Ultra-Wide camera as well, and you may seamlessly switch between your cameras while shooting the video. You can tap on the move button to focus out, or you can split on the icon to slowly switch between your camera.

8. *Audio Zoom*

The Ultra-Wide camera and the new zoom technology includes an excellent addition in the program. As you move in and out of a video, the sound zooms too!

9. *Night Setting in Camera App*

iPhone 11 has a new low-light setting that converts on automatically and works with no flash. It requires multiple images, while optical image stabilization steadies the zoom lens. Then your software aligns the images with improving for movement and removes sections with too much blur. After that, it de-sounds and enhances all the available details. What you finish up with is your final image using which you can use as it is a lot brighter.

10. *QuickTake*

QuickTake is a fresh feature approaching later in the entire year that enables you to shoot videos while you're taking photos. What's incredible is that it'll keep carefully the same frame and everything the image settings, seamlessly switching to the video mode.

That is something that's not quick to do right now. After the feature boats, all you have to do is touch and hang on the Shutter button to begin recording a video. After that, you can swipe left to lock the video if you want to capture longer videos.

11. *12MP Front side Facing Camera*

There's a new and improved camera sensor in the TrueDepth camera system. It's now a 12MP sensor with an f/2.2 aperture.

12. *Faster Face Identification with Greater Angles*

Face ID is currently 30% faster, and it works at higher perspectives. So even if the telephone is in a roundabout way looking at you right in the facial skin, Face Identification unlock will still work.

13. *Slo-mo on Front side Facing Camera*

Apple wants to make selfies something. Now you can catch slow-motion video from the front-facing camera at up to 120 fps.

14. *4K Documenting on Front side Facing Camera*

Plus, you can record 4K video on the front-facing camera at 24, 30, or 60 fps.

15. *Portrait Setting Works together with Pets*

Thanks to the way the new wide and ultra-wide cameras interact, the portrait mode on the iPhone 11 now works for pets too! That is something we've wanted since Apple launched the iPhone XR this past year with Portrait mode but limited it only to humans.

16. *Spatial Sound with Dolby Atmos*

The speakers in the iPhone 11 include 3D Spatial sound technology. It simulates audio for a far more immersive experience; the brand new iPhone also comes with Dolby Atmos' support.

17. ***Deep Fusion***

Deep Fusion is a new image control technology by Apple that will dispatch with a software update later in the Fall. It's another form of image structure technology. Apple requires four primary and four additional photos before you press the shutter button. When you press the shutter button, it requires one huge publicity picture to get as much fine detail as possible.

After that, it works pixel-by-pixel to stitch the facts collectively from all the photos in the best manner. Everything you get can be an image with an incredible level of detail.

18. ***Longer Electric battery Life than iPhone XR***

iPhone XR already had a fantastic all-day electric battery life. iPhone 11 pushes the pub further with the addition of a complete hour to the electronic battery life. That's up to 17 hours of video playback or more to 10 hours of video loading time.

19. ***New U1 Chip***

iPhone 11 has an entirely new chip called U1 that uses Ultra-Wideband technology for spacial consciousness;

this enables iPhone 11 to locate other U1 devices precisely. If you wish to share a document using AirDrop, point your iPhone at theirs, and they'll be the first in the set of the AirDrop posting screen.

20. *Toughest Cup Ever in a Smartphone*

Apple has heard your issues loud and clear. Having a back again design that is accurately milled and sculpted from an individual piece of a cup, iPhone 11 features the most robust cup ever in a smartphone; this will help protect your iPhone in the event when it drops.

21. *Improved Water-Resistance*

iPhone 11 is IP68 certified; this implies it can withstand up to 2 meters of drinking water for thirty minutes.

22. *Extended Active Range*

The extended active range feature on the iPhone 11 while documenting videos is currently designed for 4k videos at up to 60fps. Around the iPhone XR, this is limited by 30fps videos only.

23. *Gigabit-class LTE*

iPhone 11 features Gigabit-class LTE that may help you get the best rates of speed on your moves; this is a significant omission on the iPhone XR, so it's nice to see Apple finally making your way around to adding it.

24. *Wi-Fi 6*

iPhone 11 is the first new iPhone to aid the new Wi-Fi 6 standard for faster download rates of speed. Apart from this, the iPhone 11 has yet featured that you found in iPhone XR. So that it still supports cellular charging, fast charging with the optionally available 18-watt charger that should be bought individually, Dual SIM support with eSIM, and more.

iPhone 11 will dispatch with iOS 13, with support for editing and enhancing 4K videos, dark setting, and many more.

Chapter 4

How to Customize Your iPhone Mobile

Customize iPhone Ringtones & Text message Tones

The ringtones and text tones your iPhone uses to get your attention need not be exactly like everyone else's. You may make all types of changes, including changing the sound, and that means you know who's phoning or texting without even taking a glance at your phone.

- ***Change the Default Ringtone***: Your iPhone comes pre-loaded with a large number of ringtones. Change the default ringtone for all those calls to the main one you prefer the better to get notified when you experience a call to arrive. Do this by *heading to Settings -> Noises (Noises & Haptics on some models) -> Ringtone.*

- ***Set Person Ringtones***: You can assign a different ringtone for everybody in your connections list. That way, a love track can play whenever your partner calls, and you know it's them before even looking. Do that by heading to *Phone -> Connections -> tapping the individual whose ringtone you want to improve -> Edit -> Ringtone.*

- ***Get Full-Screen Photos for Incoming Phone calls***: The incoming call screen does not have to be boring. With this suggestion, you can view a fullscreen picture of the individual calling you. Go to *Mobile phone -> Connections -> touch the individual -> Edit -> Add Picture.*

- *Customize Text Tone*: Like everyone else can customize the ringtones that play for calls, you can customize the appearance like video when you get texts. Go to *Configurations* -> *Seems (Noises & Haptics on some models)* -> *Text message Tone*.

TIPS: You're not limited by the band and text tone that include the iPhone. You can purchase ringtones from Apple, and some applications help you create your tone.

Other iPhone Customisation Options

Here's an assortment of a few other different ways to customize your iPhones.

- *Delete Pre-Installed Apps*: Got a couple of applications pre-installed on your iPhone you don't use? You can delete them (well, the majority of them, anyhow)! Just use the typical way to delete apps: Touch and keep until they tremble, then tap the x on the application icon.

- *Customize Control Centre*: Control Centre has a lot more options that are apparent initially.

Customize Control Centre to get just the group of tools you want to use. Head to *Settings -> Control Centre -> Customize Settings.*

- *Install your preferred Keyboard*: The iPhone includes an excellent onscreen keypad; nevertheless, you can install third-party keyboards that add cool features, like *Google search, emojis, and GIFs, plus much more.* Get yourself a new keyboard at the App Store, then go to *Settings -> General -> Keyboard -> Keyboards.*

- *Make Siri a friend*: Choose to have Siri talk with you utilizing a man's tone of voice? It could happen. Head to *Settings -> Siri & Search -> Siri Tone of voice -> Male.* You can even go with different accents if you want.

- *Change Browser's default search engine*: Have search engines apart from Google that you'd like to use? Make it the default for those queries in Browser. Head to *Settings -> Browser -> Search Engine and making a new selection.*

45

- *Make Your Shortcuts*: If you an iPhone 11 or newer version user, you can create all sorts of cool customized gestures and shortcuts for various jobs.

- *Jailbreak Your Phone*: To get the most control over customizing your mobile phone, you can jailbreak it; this gets rid of Apple's settings over certain types of customization. Jailbreaking can cause functional problems and lessen your phone's security, but it can give more control.

Customize iPhone Home Screen

You may take a look at your iPhone home screen more than some other single screen so that it should be set up the way you want it to appear. Below are a few options for customizing your iPhone home screen.

- *Change Your Wallpaper*: You may make the image behind your applications on the home screen just about whatever you want. A favourite picture of your children or spouse or the logo design of your preferred team is a few options.

Find the wallpaper settings by heading to *Settings -> Wallpaper -> Select a New Wallpaper.*

- *Use Live or Video Wallpaper*: Want something eye-catching? Use cartoon wallpapers instead. There are a few restrictions, but this is relatively cool. *Head to Settings -> Wallpaper -> Select a New Wallpaper -> pick and choose Active or Live.*

- *Put Apps into Folders*: Organize your home screen centred on how you Utilize applications by grouping them into folders. Begin by gently tapping and securing one application until all your apps begin to tremble. Then pull and drop one application onto another to place those two applications into a folder.

- *Add Extra Webpages of Apps*: All your apps won't need to be about the same home screen. You may make individual "webpages" for different kinds of applications or different users by tapping and keeping applications or folders, then dragging them from the right side of the screen. Browse the *"Creating Web pages on iPhone"* portion of How to Manage Apps on the iPhone Home Screen to get more.

iPhone Customizations that make things Better to see

It isn't always a simple text message or onscreen items on your iPhone, but these customizations make things much simpler to see.

- **Use Screen Focus**: Do all the onscreen symbols and text message look a little too small for your eye? Screen Move magnifies your iPhone screen automatically. To Utilize this option, go to *Settings -> Screen & Brightness -> View -> Zoomed -> Collection.*

- **Change Font Size**: The default font size on your iPhone may be a little small for your eye; nevertheless, you can raise it to make reading convenient. Head to *Settings -> General -> Availability -> Larger Text message -> move the slider to On/green -> change the slider below.*

- *Use Dark mode*: If the shiny colours of the iPhone screen strain your eye, you may choose to use Dark Setting, which inverts shiny colours to darker ones. Find the essential Dark settings in *Configurations -> General -> Convenience -> Screen Accommodations -> Invert Colours*.

Customize iPhone Lock Screen

Like everyone else, you can customize your home screen; you can customize the iPhone lock screen, too. In this manner, you have control over the very first thing you see each time you wake up your phone.

- *Customize Lock Screen Wallpaper*: Exactly like on the home screen, you can transform your iPhone lock screen wallpaper to employ a picture, computer animation, or video. Browse the link within the last section for details.

- *Create a Stronger Passcode*: The much longer your passcode, the harder it is to break right into your iPhone (you are utilizing a passcode, right?). The default passcode is 4 or 6 character types (depending on your iOS version); nevertheless, you make it much longer and stronger. *Head to Settings -> Face ID (or Touch ID) & Passcode -> Change Passcode and following an instructions.*

- **Get Suggestions from Siri**: Siri can learn your practices, preferences, passions, and location and then use that information to suggest content for you. Control what Siri suggests by heading to *Configurations -> Siri & Search -> Siri Recommendations and setting the things you want to use to On/green.*

Customize iPhone Notifications

Your iPhone helpfully notifies you to understand when you have calls, text messages, emails, and other bits of information that may interest you. But those notifications can be irritating. Customize how you get notifications with these pointers.

- **Choose Your Notification Style**: The iPhone enables you to choose lots of notification styles, from simple pop-ups to a mixture of sound and text messages, and more. Find the notification options in *Settings -> Notifications -> touch the application you want to regulate -> choose Alerts, Banner Style, Noises, and more.*

- ***Group Notifications from the Same App***: Get yourself many notifications from an individual app, but won't need to see each one taking space on your screen? You can group notifications into a *"stack"* that occupies the same space as your notification. Control this on the per-app basis by heading to *Settings -> Notifications -> the application you want to regulate -> Notification Grouping.*

- ***Adobe flashes a Light for Notifications***: Unless you want to try out to get a notification, you may make the camera adobe flashlight instead. It's a delicate, but apparent, option for most situations. Set this up in *Settings -> General -> Convenience -> Hearing -> move the LED Screen for Notifications slider to On/green.*

51

- ***Get Notification Previews with Face ID***: In case your iPhone has Face ID, you can utilize it to keep the notifications private. This establishing shows a simple headline in notifications; however, when you go through the screen and get identified by Face ID, the notification expands, showing more content. Establish this by going to *Settings -> Notifications -> Show Previews -> When Unlocked.*

TIPS: That link also offers an excellent tips about using Face ID to silent alarms, and notification sounds, i.e., *"Reduce Alarm Volume and Keep Screen Shiny with Attention Awareness."*

- ***Get more information with Notification Centre Widgets***: Notification Centre not only gathers all your notifications, but it also offers up widgets, mini-versions of applications to enable you to do things without starting apps whatsoever.

Chapter 5

iOS 13 Update and Features

The iOS 13 update is here now to introduce new features to your old iPhone, offering new software perks even though you haven't upgraded to Apple's completely new iPhone. In fact, under a week after Apple launched the iOS 13 upgrade, it gave us another software revise for iPhones with the iOS 13.1 update, which comes with lots of crucial Bug fixes and many more new features.

Dark Setting is the best iOS 13 feature and the most visible change. It inverts white and light grey colors for less eye-straining dark and dark greys - at least in significant apps. In case you want to know ways to get iOS 13, we have a step-by-step guide for it, although the upgrade comes pre-installed on the iPhone 11 and iPhone 11 Pro.

The two-minute iOS 13 review

- *Dark Setting*: We have been getting the most use from the iOS 13 feature. It changes the user interface (aside from some third-party apps), exchanging white-colored and light grey colors for dark and dark grey hues. That's more enjoyable to the eye, especially during the night.

    iOS 13 pro tips: You can set routine iOS 13 Dark Setting to turn on/off at particular times, and add it as a Control Middle menu shortcut.

- *iOS 13 compatibility*: iOS 13 works with a lot of iPhones - for as long you have the iPhone 6S or iPhone SE or recent model of iPhone. Yes, which means both iPhone 5S and iPhone 6 don't make a list and are permanently trapped with iOS 12.4.1, but Apple didn't make any slashes for iOS 12, so it was just getting up in 2019. Good.

- *Photo editing and enhancing tools get advanced*:

Now, you can change up photos in 15 various ways, tweaking highlights, comparison, and shadows. It's better quality to the stage where we're starting Adobe Lightroom.

iOS 13 pro suggestion: Edits also work for video, and you may edit photos without destroying the Live Picture properties.

- *A new QuickPath keyboard*: Want to swipe on the keyboard rather than tap? It's now within. No collection comes after your finger's motion, and it's just a little challenging to get accustomed to initially, but it's nearer to what we should like about Gboard. *iOS 13 pro suggestion*: We found this most readily useful on any large Max or Plus phone.

- *FaceTime correction*: You understand that part of a FaceTime call where you take a look at your display and, for that reason, aren't taking a look at the camera? Apple uses AI to go the path of your gaze. A little creepy in theory, but exceedingly useful.

- *Face ID is way better*: We love this feature - the field of view for unlocking your phone with that person is more extensive, so taking a look at the telephone on the desk will open your iPhone up without having to lift the handset.

- *iOS 13 is not approaching to the iPad*: Tricked you. iOS 13 is purely for the iPhone (and iPod touch). iPadOS has debuted for iPad with unique efficiency features for the larger tablet screen.

- *'Find my iPhone' and 'Find my Friends' are fused*: Both apps are actually in a single **'Find My'** app, and Apple's added features that will get offline devices from other iPhones or iPads. On top of that, we got fewer timed out monitoring errors.

- *iOS 13 enhances electric battery life*: By that, people mean *'lifetime of the electric battery'* not *'time between charges'* - the new iOS 13 system is smarter at charging and can curtail the energy insight at the right times. The dark setting should help too on the iPhone OLED screen, though we're screening that.

- *Reminders get an enormous (and useful) overhaul*: A definite new design, Reminders, now permits accessories and better sorting.

- *The camera gets a huge upgrade*: Family portrait mode (if your phone supports it) will offer you more customizable light and a fresh *'High Key Mono'* mode for when you wish to appear to be you're in a Calvin Klein advert.

- *Siri sounds better*: A refined tone of voice with an increase of natural diction, Siri is a lot nicer to speak to now. You will possibly not notice it without a side-by-side assessment, but it's here.

- *New Memoji to try out*: You can include make-up, throw in Memoji stickers from the keyboard - if you are into the own toon face, there's too much to try here.

  iOS 13 pro suggestion: Stickers work on iPhone 8 and old iPhones, even though you don't possess the TrueDepth camera for moving Memoji.

- *Control Wi-Fi and Bluetooth more simply*: We love this: long-press (or 3D Touch for several iPhone models) on the Wi-Fi / Bluetooth control keys in the Control Middle, and you will access all of your connections in a single simple place.

- *Use your PS4 controller on your telephone*: You will pair your system controller to try out games in a far more immersive way. PS4 support is here now today, while Xbox One support is arriving. Ideal for Apple Arcade, right?

OK, that is the key stuff taken care of - but if you would like to learn more about small features, or simply a little more depth on what your iPhone or iPad can do, continue reading:

iOS 13.1 Update

As we've mentioned, Apple pushed out the iOS 13.1 update within weekly of officially starting iOS 13 on iPhones, and it brought lots of Bug fixes as well as some new features.

iOS 13.1 Bug fixes

The discharge notes for iOS 13.1 display how buggy the original release of iOS 13 was, with the new upgrade getting fixes for difficulties with Email, Siri not working with CarPlay, defective app symbols, and sign-in failures.

Another major issue with iOS 13 was with location permissions - Fast Company recently reported that if a user had determined never to share location details for an app, a privacy flaw changed that selection to *"Ask the next time."*

Those privacy issues are also addressed in the new iOS 13.1 release, plus a fix for a lock screen bypass Bug that could let others gain access to a user's contact list by merely making a FaceTime call and using Siri's voiceover feature to get access.

iOS 13.1 new features

We've highlighted a few of the main element new

features in the iOS 13.1 update below in greater detail, but there's more, including updated Fonts configurations and Personal Hotspot webpages. If you test beta apps, they'll now be indicated with an orange dot in iOS 13.1, and the old active bubble wallpapers that disappeared when Apple added dark mode-friendly wallpapers in iOS 13, are back again.

There's a fresh 'Peak Performance Ability' feature in the iPhone XS, iPhone XR, and the XS Max, as they're now 12 months old and could start having electric battery issues as they continue steadily to age; which means that as the battery begins to degrade, the performance management feature will be triggered to throttle the CPU, although a choice to disable this will be accessible at that time.

- **Share about ETA in Maps**

Google Maps added this a while back, and today Apple Maps users can also share their approximate time of introduction with relatives and buddies from the application itself. When you setup directions to a spot and begin the journey, a choice to 'Share about ETA' turns up at the bottom of the display screen.

Following that, you can pick the contact you want to share with your approximate time of arrival, which gets sent as an iMessage (to some other iPhone user) as a regular textual content. If Maps detects you'll likely arrive later than expected, a note will automatically be delivered to the contact to tell them you're operating late.

- **Lyrics view in Apple Music**

If you're an Apple Music customer, you'll find a new icon - just like a conversation bubble - underneath the left-hand side of the pane. When chosen, it introduces lyrics to the track you're currently hearing. The words will also automatically scroll just like a karaoke machine. Lyrics can be found only if tunes have been downloaded from Apple Music, not for songs added from an outside source via iTunes.

- **AirDrop update**

That is specific to the 2019 iPhones, taking a "spatial awareness" of the Ultra-Wideband technology in the new

U1 chip in the iPhone 11, 11 Pro, and iPhone 11 Pro Max. If you are using the latest handsets, you can AirDrop documents to other compatible iOS devices by merely pointing towards these devices, meaning both devices know about their position following each other.

- **Automation tabs in Shortcuts**

The Shortcuts application is becoming smarter, with a less strenuous way to create new routines. For instance, you can result in turning off your early morning routine by establishing a Shortcut that makes your drive to focus on Maps, introduces your day's visits on Calendar, etc.

You can set a period for every trigger, meaning Maps will launch automatically at, say, 10 am as you prepare to set off.

iOS 13 compatibility list

- iOS 13 works with iPhone 6S / iPhone SE or later.

- iOS 13 isn't appropriate for iPhone 5S, iPhone 6, iPhone 6 Plus

iOS 13 compatibility requires an iPhone from the last four years; this means cell phones like the iPhone 6 will not be getting iOS 13 - if you have such a device, you will be stuck with iOS 12.4.1 forever.

You will need an iPhone 6S, iPhone 6S Plus or iPhone SE or later to set up iOS 13. With iPadOS, while different, you will need an iPhone Air 2 or iPad mini 4 or later.

The iPhone SE fits into an odd category, as they have iPhone 6 era specs, but arrived following the iPhone 6S. Don't be concerned; everyone's favorite little iPhone is sure to get iOS 13. iOS 13 works with just one single iPod device - the latest version. No real surprise, the new iPod touch 7th gen is the only device of its course that gets iOS 13 support.

iOS 13 Dark Mode

- Overdue Dark Setting is approaching to iOS 13 and iPadOS

- We saw macOS get a system-wide Dark Setting in 2018

- Shortcut to black-and-dark-grey UI stays in charge Center.

Dark Setting in iOS 13 a system-wide, meaning it changes the hues from white-colored and light grey to dark and dark grey on all supported apps. It's a useful feature if you are making use of your iPhone during the night and want to avoid white-colored hues glowing in that person. It could also save electric battery life on the OLED-equipped iPhones, from the iPhone X onward. Apple didn't discuss this whatsoever, but we realize that OLED shows fundamentally 'change off' pixels when making blacks.

Turning on iOS 13 Dark Setting can be carried out in Control Center inside the Screen split (right next to the night time Change and True Firmness toggle), relating to Apple, or you can set it automatically to carefully turn on during the night through a routine or custom time.

The yellow-tinting Night time Change mode finally gets a bright-light dimming companion, and a lot of individuals couldn't be happier.

iOS 13 offers 'FaceTime attention correction'

There's a choice for FaceTime Attention Modification, and it's as crazy as it seems. What does it do exactly? It creates it such that it shows up as though you're looking directly into the front-facing camera throughout a FaceTime video call if you are taking a look at the adjacent display. That sidetracked look is a thing of days gone by soon.

iOS 13 on iPad is iPadOS, and it's a big change

A number of the most significant changes for iOS 13 on the iPad are actually to arrive at a revised called iPadOS. Apple is signaling that the iPad needs its platform, which is a significant improvement to your iPad workflow; you start with the home display screen redesign. Pinned Widgets, enables you to add widgets from the Today View display (that left-mode display screen on your iPhone and iPad). Up to now, it's iPad-exclusive, rather than arriving at iOS13 for the iPhone.

Split Over enables you to have multiple applications open and routine through them like *Rolodex*. You can even love to preview all of them simultaneously with a swipe gesture, similar to the new menu on many mobile phones and tablets; it's multi-tasking doable.

Break up View has been improved to enable you to open one application on both edges of the display (it wasn't possible before), and Apple demoed this by showing Records side-by-side with Notes. You can even pair an application with an increase of than one application - so now Safari can be paired with Pages in a single space, and Safari can be paired with Mail in another.

App Expose is not used to the iPad software, permitting you to see all the space you have open up. There's an App Expose icon on the Dock, needing only a single press to find yourself in the convenient overview setting. New duplicate, paste and undo gestures are approaching iPadOS. Three fingertips scrunched down was proven to duplicate text, three fingertips expanding (on the contrary direction) dropped the written text on the web page, and slipping three fingers over the display screen undo the last action. We'll have to observe how this performs when the program lands.

Apple's keypad can float around the display in a smaller form, and it's debuting a swiping gesture keypad, which it calls *QuickPath Typing*. There's also more keypad shortcuts (too little shortcuts was a problem we'd like talk about earlier iOS variations).

iOS 13 includes a QuickPath keyboard

With iOS 13, Apple's default QuickType keyboard will be incorporating swipe-to-type, a favorite way of sliding over the keyboard to create words. We've used this in prior iOS keypad extensions like **Google's Gboard** and **SwiftKey**.

You should use the QuickType and QuickPath ways of typing interchangeably, therefore far supported languages include *English, Simplified Chinese, Spanish, German, French, Italian, and Portuguese* is currently included.

iOS 13 debuts new 'Find My' app

Apple combined Find My Friends and discover My iPhone in iOS 13, and the union enables you to locate friends and family and missing devices with a faster, easier-to-use user interface. What's nice is it use a crowd-sourced encrypted Bluetooth transmission to help you find devices that are not linked to Wi-Fi or mobile. That's mostly a massive help for Macs, but it might also assist with an iPhone in rare circumstances, too.

On top of that, while Find My Friends didn't always work for all of us, Apple appears to be making a broader drive to get location monitoring right with this new iOS 13 application now in the limelight.

iOS 13 makes your old iPhone faster, go longer

More folks are keeping their iPhones for longer, and that is something Apple appears to recognize - and the business is accelerating iOS 13 to support them.

The main iOS 13 stats: application start speed is up to

doubly fast according to Apple, and Face ID unlocking will be 30% faster than before. Apple also found ways to make application downloads smaller, up to 60% normally; iOS 12 provided us a faster upgrade, and iOS 13 appears to build upon that.

Electric battery life is also something Apple is tackling this season. Its goal is to reduce the pace of battery aging by decreasing the time your iPhone usually spends fully billed. iOS 13 is meant to study from your daily charging regular so that it can wait around to complete charging past 80% until you should employ it.

Reminders gets a large overhaul

Of all built-in apps, Reminders has gotten the largest iOS revamp. It's better structured and includes shortcuts, which make it simpler to add reminders. Big, colour-coded control keys for Today, Scheduled, All and Flagged categories provide you with a much better oversight of your pressing jobs, while the keypad if you are in this application has a top-line Quick Toolbar that functions as a shortcut to easily add times, locations, flags, photos and scanned documents.

Is it making programs in Communications? Siri will part of to suggest reminders that may be created, such as a personal associate who chimes in at the right times.

Camera and portrait Mode changes

The iOS 13 offers significant changes to camera features; you start with helping you to change the intensity of light in Family portrait Setting, which is something we've wanted for some time. The family portrait setting is also obtaining a new monochromatic impact called *High-Key Mono*. The Photos gallery is now what Apple called *"a journal you will ever have,"* with a new tab made to document your very best photos by day, month, and year. You will also have significantly more pinch regulates to focus in and from the Photos gallery.

Now you can do something that a lot of folks have been crying out for with an iPhone - change the aspect percentage of the picture you ingest the camera app; which means square options, or 16:9 even, it's there in the configurations - although when you export the images of the telephone, the files remain in the initial 4:3 format.

Photo editing and enhancing is refined with iOS 13, adding adjusting controls and filter systems, as the video editing and enhancing part mirrors this almost entirely: almost every picture tool and impact - including filter systems, rotating, and cropping - helps it be to video. If you are bad at trying out the video, there'll even be a 'Car' realignment button.

New Siri tone of voice sounds more natural

A fresh Siri voice debuts with iOS 13, and it sounds more natural than before - we've heard an example, and the tone is the same, but it sounds less robotic. It uses advanced neural textual content-to-conversation technology, according to Apple, and you will particularly notice this when Siri says much longer phrases, like reading the Apple Information aloud or answering knowledge questions.

The timing is good because Siri can also do much more sharing if you wear AirPods - Siri can read incoming communications and pipe them through the buds, which is convenient. *Yet another new Siri benefit:* your tone of voice helper on AirPod will understand the voices of the many family members in your house; this will mean, for example, that requesting "What's on my Calendar?" won't share about someone else's unimportant information.

Memoji gets make-up, Text messages get info sharing

Apple has put more of *'Me personally'* is Memoji, allowing one trillion configurations: new hairstyles, headwear, make-up, and piercings to mention a few categories. Good examples on the WWDC stage demonstrated that these customized Animoji masks enable such granular accessories fine detail as eyeshadow, brackets and even AirPods.

Memoji Stickers are something completely new - iOS 13 brings more iPhone and iPad users into the Memoji fold, TrueDepth camera, or not. You can customize a Memoji, and iOS 13 will automatically produce a fun-looking sticker pack that lives in a sub-menu on the keypad, used in Messages, Email, and third-party apps.

You can share your individualized Memoji with friends through *iMessage*, but only once you give them access. The same pertains to posting your name and picture with contacts, and that means you can be selected how people see your name, for example. Relating to Apple, you can decide whether you want your profile distributed to everyone, with only your connections, or simply once.

Chapter 6

How to Create & Use iPhone 11 Shortcuts

How to Put in a Virtual Home Button to the iPhone

In respect to get a virtual Home button configured, you first have to allow the home button itself. Here's how:

- Touch *Settings*.

- Touch *General*.

- Touch *Accessibility*.

- Touch *AssistiveTouch*.

- Move the *AssistiveTouch* slider to On/green. The digital Home button shows up on your screen.

- Position the button anywhere on your screen using drag and drop.

- Make the button pretty much transparent utilizing the Idle Opacity slider.

- Touch the button to see its default menu.

How to Customize the Virtual Home Button Menu

To change the number of shortcuts and the precise ones that exist in the default menu:

- Around the *Assistive Touch* screen, tap Customize Top Level Menu.

- Change the number of icons shown in the very best Level Menu with the plus and minus control keys at the bottom of the screen. The minimum volume of options is 1; the utmost is 8. Each icon represents a different shortcut.

- To improve a shortcut, touch the icon you want to improve.

- Tap one of the available shortcuts from the list that appears.

- Touch Done to save the change. It replaces the shortcut you have chosen.

- If you decide you want to return to the default group of options, touch Reset.

How to Add Custom Activities to the Virtual Home Button

Now that you understand how to include the virtual Home button and configure the menu, it is time to get to the nice stuff: custom shortcuts. As being a physical Home button, the digital button can be configured to react differently based on how you touch it. Some tips about what you must do:

Within the *AssistiveTouch* screen, go directly to the Custom Actions section. For that section, touch the action that you would like to use to result in the new shortcut. Your alternatives are:

- *Single-Touch*: The original single click of the home button. In cases like this, it's an individual touch on the digital button.

- *Double-Touch*: Two quick touches on the button; if you choose this, you can also control the Timeout establishing (i.e., the time allowed between touches) if additional time goes by between touches, the iPhone goodies them as two solitary touches, not a double-touch.

- **Long Press**: Touch and contain the virtual Home button. If you choose this, you can also configure a Duration, which sets how long you will need to press the screen because of this feature to be triggered.

- **3D Touch**: The 3D Touch screen on modern iPhones lets the screen respond differently based on how hard you press it. Utilize this option to have the digital Home button react to hard presses.

Whichever action you touch, each screen presents several options for shortcuts that you can assign to the action. They are especially cool because they change actions that may normally require pressing multiple control keys into an individual touch.

Most shortcuts are self-explanatory, such as Siri, Screenshot, or Volume Up, but a few need description:

- **Convenience Shortcut**: This shortcut may be used to cause all types of convenience features, such as inverting colours for users with eyesight impairment, turning on VoiceOver, and zooming in on the screen.

- *Shaking*: Choose this, and the iPhone responds to a button touch as if an individual shook the telephone. Shake pays for undoing certain activities, particularly if physical issues prevent you from shaking the telephone.

- *Pinch*: Performs the same as a pinch gesture on the iPhone's screen, which pays for people who've impairments that produce pinching hard or impossible.

- *SOS*: This button allows the iPhone's Emergency SOS feature, which causes a loud sound to alert others that you might need help and a call to Emergency services.

- *Analytics*: This feature starts the gathering of Assistive Touch diagnostics.

Chapter 7

Recommended iPhone Applications

<u>Spark</u>: Best Email App for iPhone 11

If you centre on iOS apps, you would understand that email has taken on something similar to the role of the antagonist in the wonderful world of iOS. App designers appear to know that everyone needs a better email platform, and they want an application to resolve their issues. Controlling email is just a little less stressful if you are using ***Spark*** as you would find features to suit your needs, such as; sending, snoozing email messages, and a good inbox that only notifies you of important email messages.

Below are the things you'd like about this application:

- The app is simple to use and socially friendly.

- Swipe-based interaction allows for one-handed operation.

What You may not like about it:

- No filter systems for automatically sorting email messages.

- The app does not have a way of controlling messages in batches.

Things: The best "To-do manager" for the iPhone 11

To-do manager applications are a packed field, and the application called *"Things"* isn't the only good one, and it is also not the only *to-do manager* on this list, but it's a carefully reliable tool, seated between control and hardy. The application provides the ideal levels of both control and hardy, without mind-boggling users to dials and without dropping essential features.

Things you'd like about this application:

- This app has a simplified interface that reduces stress when adding and completing the task.

- Tasks can be added from iOS with the sheet extension.

What you may not like are:

- Repeating tasks and deadlines can be buggy.

- Tasks can't be put into the calendar automatically.

<u>OmniCentre</u>: Best GTD-compatible To-Do App for iPhone 11

Like *"Things,"* **OmniCentre** is a favourite and well-designed to-do manager; however, they have a different group of priorities. Where **Things** attempts to remain simple and straightforward, **OmniCentre** is feature-rich and robust.

The application fully integrates with the **"Getting Things Done"** approach to task management called **GTD**, and this method stimulates users to jot down any duties they have, as well as almost all their associated information and scheduling. GTD users would finish up spending a great deal of time on leading end arranging work; because of this, the software takes a robust feature collection to implement all areas of the GTD process.

Things you'd like about this application:

- Most effective to-do list manager available.

- Can participate in virtually any task management style.

What you may not like:

- Sacrifices simpleness and usability for power and versatility.

Agenda: Best iPhone 11 App for Busy Notice Takers

Agenda requires a different spin on the notes application than almost every other application; its also known as *"date centred notice taking app."* Records are structured by task and day, and the times are a large part of the Agenda. Instead of merely collecting your jotting into a collection, Agenda creates a to-do list from *"things,"* with tight time integration, Agenda makes an operating journaling app and an able to-do manager and general iPhone 11 note-taking app. The day and note mixture seems apparent, but Agenda is the first iOS note-taking application to perform this mixture effectively.

It's a "to-do manager" and also a note-taking application with some calendar features, which enables seeing every information in a single place with one perspective and only one app. The application is also highly practical in the freeform, which may be uncommon in flagship apps. The beauty of the app *"Agenda"* comes out when using Pencil support, but for the present time, we'll have to turn to the iPad Pro for the feature.

Things you'd like about this application:

- Note-taking small tweaks can improve many workflows.

- The time-based organization fits most users; mental types of information organization.

What you may not like:

- Slow app release can limit how quickly you can write down a note.

1Password: *Best iPhone 11 App for Security password Management*

Using the auto-fill in iOS 13, **1Password** is as near to perfect as we have in a password manager. The Face ID authentication isn't unique to the iPhone 11 alone, but access Face ID makes the application better and simpler to use, which is an uncommon combination of accomplishments to reach concurrently.

Things you'd like about this application:

- Finding and copying usernames and passwords is extremely easy.

- Secure document storage space means *1Password* can gather all of your secure information in a single place.

- Auto-fill support finally makes security password management as easy as typing your security password.

What you may not like:

- No free version.

- The paid version uses membership pricing.

Twitterific: Best Tweets App For iPhone 11

Twitter is probably not the most exceptional sociable media system, but it's still one of the very most popular internet sites around, and like many internet sites, Twitter's default application is disappointingly bad.

Unfortunately, Twitter does lately nerf third-party Twitter clients. Third-party applications won't receive real-time stream notifications, significantly reducing the effectiveness of the applications; this move seems to pressure users to go to the native app, but considering its many defects, Twitterific and applications like it remain better.

Things you'd like about this application:

- Improves Twitter's visual demonstration dramatically.

- Includes smart and powerful features that make Twitter simpler to use.

What you may not like:

- Some organizational options are initially unintuitive.

- Twitter has purposefully knee-capped a good number of third-party apps, and Twitterific is no defence to those results.

Overcast: **Best iPhone 11 App for Podcasts**

Overcast is the best application you may use to hear podcasts. The app's user interface is considered carefully for maximal consumer performance, with features like "Smart Rate" which helps to intelligently manages a podcast's playback speed to shorten silences without accelerating speech, while Tone of voice Boost offers a pre-built EQ curve made to amplify voices, which is ideal for a loud hearing environment.

Things you'd like about this application:

- Thoughtfully designed interface for sorting and hearing podcasts.

- Features like Smart Speed and Queue playlists are invaluable once you're used to them.

- Active developer centred on avoiding an unhealthy user experience concerning monetization.

What you may not like;

- It most definitely doesn't seem to go nicely with the iOS lock screen.

Apollo: **Best iPhone 11 App for Reddit**

If you're thinking about *Reddit*, you would want to see the website beyond the third-party app. The application has improved, sure, but it's still kilometres behind third-party offerings.

Apollo is the best of the number as it pertains to Reddit clients, conquering out past champions like "Narwhal." Development is continuous and ongoing, with many improvements from the dev in the app's subreddit.

The swipe-based navigation would continue to work on any iPhone, of course, but it dovetails nicely with the iPhone 11's application switching behaviour. The real black setting is also a delicacy for OLED screens.

Things you'd like about this application:

- Effortlessly handles an enormous variety of media.

- Well developed UI makes navigation easy.

- No ads in virtually any version of the app.

What you may not like:

- Sometimes is suffering from annoying and lingering bugs.

Focos: Best iPhone 11 App for Editing and enhancing Portrait Setting Photos

By default, the iPhone 11's Family portrait Mode is a one-and-done process; you take the picture, and the blur is applied. iOS doesn't give a built-in way for editing and enhancing the Picture Setting effect following the fact. Focos fills the space, creating a tool to tweak both degrees of shadow and the blur face mask. It mimics the result you'd see when modifying a zoom lens' physical aperture. More magically, you can also change the centre point following the shot by recreating the blurred cover up on the different object, or by hand adjusting the result on the image's depth face mask instantly.

Things you'd like about this application:

- The most effective approach to manipulating Portrait Mode's depth-of-field effect.

- The depth map is a distinctive feature to help visualize blur.

What you may not like:

- Simple to make images look over-processed.

- Only about the centre, 50% of the blur range looks natural.

Halide: Best iPhone 11 App for Natural Photos

Distinctively, *Halide* sticks essential info in the iPhone 11's "ear." It embeds a live histogram for image evaluation; could it be precious? Nearly, but Halide is a near-perfect picture taking software besides that offering feature.

The settings are ideally positioned and configured, the RAW catch is pixel-perfect, and navigation within the application is easy and immediately understandable. If you are seriously interested in taking photos on your iPhone 11, *Halide* is the best camera application for iOS.

Things you'd like about this application:

- Low handling power for iPhone photos.

- The broadest toolset of any iOS image editing and enhancing the app.

What you may not like:

- It can overwhelm first-time users using its degree of control.

Euclidean Lands: The Top-rated AR Puzzle Game for iPhone 11

Augmented reality applications haven't yet found their killer use. But AR gambling takes great benefit from lots of the iPhone 11's features.

Euclidean Lands is a short fun puzzler that calls for the full benefit of AR's potential. Similar to Monument Valley, players manipulate the play space to produce new pathways through puzzle designs, guiding their avatar to the finish of the maze. The overall game begins easy; nevertheless, you might be scratching your head just a little by the end.

Things you'd like in this application:

- Challenging and attractive puzzle levels that take benefit of AR's unique features.

What you may not like:

- Disappointingly short.

- The core game auto technician feels very familiar.

Giphy World: *Best AR Messaging App for iPhone 11*

Plenty of applications have tried to usurp Snapchat as an AR messaging system. While Snapchat might maintain a weakened condition because of self-inflicted damage, it isn't eliminated yet. But if it can decrease, Giphy World is a great replacement.

Things you'd like about this application:

- Simple to create fun and funny images from provided assets.

- Content isn't locked inside the Giphy app.

What you may not like:

- Object place and processing speed are inferior compared to Snapchat's.

Jig Space: *Best Usage of AR for Education on iPhone 11*

Learning with holograms is one particular thing you regularly see in sci-fi movies; with *Jig Space* and *augmented* actuality, that kind of thing is now possible in our daily lives. You should use the application to find out about various topics, including what sort of lock works, manipulating every part of the system, and looking at it from alternative perspectives. Jig Space requires the benefit of AR's three sizes effectively, and the low-poly models AR has bound not to harm the grade of the visualizations.

Things you'd like about this application:

- Takes benefit of AR's advantages for a good cause.
- A substantial assortment of "jigs" charges is free.

What you may not like:

- Accompanying captions are occasionally disappointingly shallow.

Nighttime Sky: Best Late-Night Outside Companion App

Directing out constellations is much more fun if you are

not making them up as you decide to go. *Evening Sky* was the main augmented-reality style application to seem on iOS. It shows just how for others on the system wanting to mimic its success, but it's remained dominant nevertheless.

Things you'd like about this application:

- It enhances the natural world with technology.

- It improves the star-gazing experience for both children and adults.

What you may not like:

- Large image units mean large camera motions are stiff and jerky.

Inkhunter: Most Readily Useful AR Gimmick on iOS

There's something distinctively exotic about checking out new tattoos by yourself. *Inkhunter* uses the energy of augmented truth to generate short-term digital symbols you can construct on the body and screenshot. You should use the built-in adobe flash, pull your designs, or import property from somewhere else to project on your skin.

Things you'd like about this application:

- Fun and book application idea that's useful.

What you may not like:

- Is suffering from AR's existing restrictions in surface matching.

Chapter 8

iPhone 11 Gestures You Should Know

Just like the iPhone 7 launched in 2017, the iPhone 11 doesn't include a physical home button, instead deciding on gestures to regulate the new user interface. It would require a couple of days to get used to the change but stay with it. By day three, you'll question how you ever coped without it, and using an "old" iPhone would appear old and antiquated.

1. **Unlock your iPhone 11:** Go through the phone and swipe up from underneath the screen. It truly is that easy, and also you don't need to hold back for the padlock icon at the very top to improve to the unlock visual before swiping up.

2. **Touch to wake:** Tap on your iPhone 11 screen when it's off to wake it up and find out what notifications you have. To unlock it with FaceID, you'll still have to set it up.

3. **Back to the Homescreen:** Whatever application

you are in, if you would like to return to the Home screen, swipe up from underneath of the screen. If you're within an application that is operating scenery, you'll need to keep in mind slipping up from underneath the screen (i.e., the medial side) rather than where the Home button used to be.

4. **Have a screenshot:** Press the power button and the volume up button together quickly, and it would snap a screenshot of whatever is on the screen.

5. **Addressing Control Centre:** It used to be always a swipe up, now it's a swipe down from the very best right of the screen. Even if your iPhone doesn't have 3D Touch, you can still long-press on the symbols to gain usage of further configurations within each icon.

6. **Accessing open up apps:** Previously, you raise tapped on the home button to uncover what apps you'd open. You now swipe up and then pause with your finger on the screen. After that, you can see the applications you have opened up in the

order you opened them.

7. **Launch Siri:** When you may use the "Hey Siri" hot term to awaken Apple's digital associate, there are still ways to release the function utilizing a button press. Press and contain the wake/rest button on the right aspect of the phone before Siri interface pops-up on screen.

8. **Switch your phone off:** Because long-pressing the wake/rest button launches Siri now, there's a fresh way for switching the phone off. To take action, you would need to press and contain the wake/rest button and the volume down button at the same time. Now glide to power off.

9. **Release Apple Pay:** Again, the wake/rest button is the main element here. Double touch it, and it would talk about your Apple Budget, then scan that person, and it'll request you to keep your phone near to the payment machine.

10. **Gain access to widgets on the lock screen:** Swipe from still left to directly on your lock screen, ideal

for checking your activity bands.

Using Memoji

- **Create your Memoji:** Open up Messages and begin a new meaning. Touch the tiny monkey icon above the keypad, and then strike the "+" button to generate your personality. You would customize face form, skin tone, curly hair colour, eye, jewellery, plus much more.

- **Use your Memoji/Animoji in a FaceTime call:** Take up a FaceTime call, then press the tiny star icon underneath the corner. Now, tap the Memoji you want to use.

- **Memoji your selfies:** So, if you select your Memoji face, preferably to your real to life face, you can send selfies with the Memoji changing your head in Messages. Take up a new message and touch the camera icon, and then press that top button. Now choose the Animoji option by tapping that monkey's mind again. Choose your Memoji and tap the '*X*,' not the "done" button, and then take your picture.

- **Record a Memoji video:** Sadly, Memoji isn't available as a choice in the camera app, but that doesn't mean you can't record one. Much like the picture selfie, go to communications, touch on the camera icon and then slip to video and then tap on the superstar. Weight the Animoji or your Memoji, and off you decide to go.

iOS 13 iPhone 11 Notification Tips

- *Notifications collection to provide quietly*: If you're worried that you would be getting way too many notifications, you can place the way they deliver with an app by application basis. Swipe left when you've got a notification on the Lock screen and touch on Manage. Touch Deliver Quietly. Calm notifications come in Notification Centre, but do not show up on the Lock screen, play audio, present a banner or badge the application icon. You've just surely got to be sure you check every once in a while.

- ***Switch off notifications from an app***: Same method as the "Deliver Quietly" feature, other than you tap the "Switch off..." option.

- ***Open up Notification Centre on Lock screen***: From your lock screen, swipe up from the center of the screen, and you would visit a long set of earlier notifications if you have any.

- ***Check Notifications anytime***: To check on your Notifications anytime, swipe down from the very best left part of the screen to reveal them.

Using Screen Time

- ***Checking your Screen Time***: You can examine how you've been making use of your phone with the new Screen Time feature in iOS 13. You'll find the reviews in *Configurations > Screen Time.*

- ***Scheduled Downtime:*** If you want just a little help making use of your mobile phone less, you can restrict what applications you utilize when. Check out Settings > Screen Time and choose the

Downtime option. Toggle the change to the "on" position and choose to routine a period when only specific applications and calls are allowed. It's ideal for preventing you or your children from using their cell phones after an arranged time, for example.

- ***Set application limits***: App Limitations enable you to choose which group of applications you want to include a period limit to. Choose the category and then "add" before choosing a period limit and striking "plans."

- ***Choose "always allowed" apps***: However, you might be willing to lock down your phone to avoid you utilizing it, that's no good if most of your way of getting in touch with people is via an application that gets locked away. Utilize this feature always to allow certain applications whatever limitations you apply.

- ***Content & Personal privacy limitations***: This section is also within the primary Screen Time configurations menu and particularly useful if you are a mother or father with kids who use iOS devices. Utilizing it, you can restrict all types of content and options, including iTunes and in-app buys, location services, advertising, etc. It's worth looking at.

Siri shortcuts

- *Siri Shortcuts*: There are several little "help" the iPhone 11 offers via Siri Shortcuts. To start to see the ones recommended for you, go to *Configurations > Siri & Search* and choose what you think would be helpful from the automatically produced suggestions. Touch "all shortcuts" to see more. If you wish to install specific "shortcuts" for a variety of different applications that aren't recommended by the iPhone, you can do this by downloading the dedicated Siri Shortcuts.

iPhone 11 Control Centre Tips

- *Add new handles*: Just like the previous version of

iOS, you can include and remove handles from Control Centre. Check out *Configurations > Control Centre > Customize Handles* and then choose which settings you would like to add.

- *Reorganize handles*: To improve the order of these settings, you've added, touch, and contain the three-bar menu on the right of whichever control you would like to move, then move it along the list to wherever you would like it to be.

- *Expand handles*: Some settings may become full screen, press harder on the control you want to expand, and it will fill the screen.

- *Activate screen recording*: Among the new options, you can include regulating Centre is Screen Recording. Be sure you add the control, then open up Control Centre and press the icon that appears like an excellent white circle in the thin white band. To any extent further, it'll record everything that occurs on your screen. Press the control again if you are done, and it will save a video to your Photos application automatically.

- *Adjust light/screen brightness*: You can activate your camera adobe flash, utilizing it as a torch by starting Control Centre and tapping on the torch icon. If you wish to adjust the lighting, power press the icon, then adapt the full-screen slider that shows up.

- *Quickly switch where a sound is played*: One cool feature is the capability to change where music is playing. While music is playing, through Apple Music, Spotify, or wherever, press on the music control or touch the tiny icon in the very best part of the music control; this introduces a pop-up screening available devices that you can play through; this may be linked earphones, a Bluetooth loudspeaker, Apple Television, your iPhone, or any AirPlay device.

- *Set an instant timer*: Rather than going to the timer app, you can force press on the timer icon, then glide up or down on the full-screen to create a timer from about a minute to two hours long.

- *How to gain access to HomeKit devices*: Open up Control Centre and then tap on the tiny icon that appears like a home.

iPhone 11 Photos and Camera Tips

- *Enable/disable Smart HDR*: Among the new iPhone's camera advancements is HDR, which helps boost colors, light, and detail in hard light conditions. It's on by default, but if you would like to get it turned on or off, you manually can check out *Settings > Camera and discover the Smart HDR toggle change.*

- *Keep a standard photograph with HDR*: Right under the Smart HDR toggle is a "Keep Normal Photo" option, which would save a regular, no HDR version of your picture as well as the Smart HDR photo.

- *Portrait Lights*: To take Portrait Setting shots with artificial lights, first go to capture in Family portrait mode. Portrait Setting only works for people on the iPhone 11 when capturing with the rear-facing camera. To choose your Portrait Setting capturing style, press and hang on the screen where it says "DAYLIGHT" and then move your finger to the right.

- ***Edit Portrait Lights after taking pictures***: Open up any Family portrait shot in Photos and then tap "edit." After another or two, you will see the light effect icon at the bottom of the image, touch it, and swipe just as you did when shooting the picture.

- ***Edit Portrait setting Depth***: Using the new iPhone 11, you can modify the blur impact after shooting the Portrait shot. Check out Photos and choose the picture you want to regulate, then select "edit." You will see a depth slider at the bottom of the screen. Swipe to boost the blur strength, swipe left to diminish it.

- ***How exactly to Merge People in Photos app***: Photos in iOS can check out your photos and identify people and places. If you discover that the application has chosen the same person, but says they vary, you can combine the albums collectively. To get this done, go directly to the Photos application > Albums and choose People & Places. Touch on the term "Select" at the very top right of the screen and then select the images of individuals you want to merge, then tap "merge."

- ***Remove people in Photos app***: Head to Photos App, Albums, and choose People & Places. To eliminate tap on "Choose" and then tap on individuals, you do not want to see before tapping on "Remove" underneath still left of your iPhone screen.

iPhone 11: Keyboard Tips

- *Go one-handed*: iOS 13's QuickType keypad enables you to type one-handed, which is fantastic on the larger devices like the iPhone 11 and XS Greatest extent. Press and contain the emoji or world icon and then keypad configurations. Select either the still left or right-sided keypad. It shrinks the keyboard and techniques it to 1 aspect of the screen. Get back to full size by tapping the tiny arrow.

- *Use your keyboard as a trackpad*: Previously, with 3D Touch shows, you utilize the keyboard area as a trackpad to go the cursor on the screen. You'll still can, but it works just a little in a different way here, rather than pressure pressing anywhere on the keypad, press, and hangs on the spacebar instead.

Face ID Tips

- ***Adding another in-person ID***: if you regularly change appearance now, you can put in a second In person ID to state the iPhone 11 getting puzzled. That is also really useful if you would like to add your lover to allow them to use your mobile phone while you're traveling, for example.

iPhone 11: Screen Tips

- ***Standard or Zoomed screen***: Since iPhone 6 Plus, you've had the opportunity to select from two quality options. You can transform the screen settings from Standard or Zoomed on the iPhone 11 too. To change between your two - if you have changed your mind after set up - go to *Configurations > Screen & Lighting > Screen Focus and choose Standard or Zoomed.*

- ***Enable True Tone screen***: If you didn't get it done

at the step, you could transform it anytime. To get the iPhone's screen to automatically change its color balance and heat to complement the background light in the area, check out Control Centre and push press the screen lighting slider. Now touch the True Firmness button. You can even go to *Configurations > Screen and Lighting and toggle the "True Shade" switch.*

iPhone 11 Battery Tips

- *Check your average battery consumption*: In iOS 13, you can check out Settings > Battery, and you will see two graphs. One shows the electric battery level; the other shows your screen on and screen off activity. You would find two tabs. One shows your last day; the other turns up to fourteen days; this way, you can view how energetic your phone battery strength and breakdowns screening your average screen on and off times show under the graphs.

- *Enable Low-Power Mode*: The reduced Power

Mode (Settings > Electric battery) enables you to reduce power consumption. The feature disables or lessens background application refresh, auto-downloads, email fetch, and more (when allowed). You can turn it on at any point, or you are prompted to carefully turn it on at the 20 and 10 % notification markers. You can even put in control to regulate Centre and get access to it quickly by swiping up to gain access to Control Centre and tapping on the electric battery icon.

- *Find electric battery guzzling apps*: iOS specifically lets you know which apps are employing the most power. Head to Configurations > Electric battery and then scroll right down to the section that provides you with an in-depth look at all of your battery-guzzling apps.

- *Check your battery via the Electric battery widget*: Inside the widgets in Today's view, some cards enable you to start to see the battery life staying in your iPhone, Apple Watch, and linked headphones. Just swipe from left to directly on your Home screen to access your Today view and scroll until you start to see the "Batteries" widget.

- *Charge wirelessly*: To utilize the iPhone's wifi charging capabilities, buy a radio charger. Any Qi charger will continue to work, but to charge more effectively, you will need one optimized for Apple's 7.5W charging.

- *Fast charge it*: When you have a 29W, 61W, or 87W USB Type-C power adapter for a MacBook, you can plug in your iPhone 11 Pro utilizing a Type-C to Lightning wire watching it charge quickly. Up to 50 % in thirty minutes.

Chapter 9

How to unlock its Photographic Potential

Taking photos in the iPhone's default camera application is pretty simple and straightforward - in fact, almost too simple for individuals who need to get a little more creative using their shots. Well, that's all transformed on the iPhone 11 and iPhone 11 Pro, which not only brings a fresh wide-angle zoom lens but a pleasant assisting of new software features that you should explore.

The difficulty is, a few of these aren't immediately apparent, and it's not necessarily clear just how to take benefit of the excess photographic power stored in your shiny new iPhone.

That's why we've come up with this beginner guide for the iPhone 11 and iPhone 11 Pro's digital cameras, to get a solid foothold and springtime towards Instagram greatness. Continue reading and get snapping.

1. *Figure out how to look beyond your frame*

When shooting the typical (26mm comparative) zoom lens, the iPhone 11 and iPhone 11 Pro use the wide-angle zoom lens showing you what's happening beyond your frame, a little just like a range-finder camera. Those digital cameras have always been popular with professional road photographers because they enable you to nail the precise moment when a fascinating character walks into the frame.

You shouldn't do anything to create this up - endure your iPhone 11 with the camera application open and point it towards the scene to view it in action. Look for a photogenic background like a vacant road, then use the wide-angle preview to time as soon as your subject matter enters the shot. Want to keep the wide-angle view of your picture carefully.

2. *Adjust your compositions*

Here's another fun new feature on the iPhone 11 and iPhone 11 Pro that's great if you can't quite determine the ultimate way to take a picture. You'll need to go to the main configurations, wherein the Camera section; you'll find an option called "*Composition.*" If you enable "Photos Catch Outside the Framework," the camera will record two photos at the same time - one using the wide-angle zoom lens, and another using the typical angle.

There are always a few facts to consider when working with this nifty trick. First is that you'll have to take in the HEIF format, which isn't always dealt with well by non-iOS devices. Also, the broader position picture will be erased if it's not used within thirty days, so you'll have to be reasonably quick with your editing and enhancing.

To get the wide-angle view of the shot, tap *'Edit'* within the photo, then your cropping icon, then press the three dots button in the very best right and choose "Use Content Beyond your Frame."

3. *Manage HDR*

The iPhone 11 and iPhone 11 Pro include Smart HDR, which is started up by default; this automatically detects the light levels in your picture and protect both shows and shadows for a far more balanced image.

More often than not, you will see occasions when challenging conditions lead to a graphic, which is nearly right. If you'd favour less processed photos to edit within an application like Lightroom, check out the configurations menu, find the Camera section, then switch off Smart HDR.

The great thing concerning this is it doesn't eliminate using Smart HDR for several scenes - in the Camera application, you'll now see an HDR button at the very top to turn it On/Off. It just means your default capturing will be without Smart HDR's sometimes overzealous processing.

4. <u>Reach grips with Night Mode</u>

Night mode is a new feature for the iPhone 11 and iPhone 11 Pro - and it's something we've been waiting around to see in a while. It's not an ardent setting you can opt for - instead, it'll activate automatically when the iPhone detects that ambient light conditions are on the reduced side.

Nevertheless, you can still have little control over it once it is used; tap the night time setting icon at the left, and you may use a split to choose a faster shutter speed if it's brighter than the telephone realizes, or leave it on Car - or you can also choose to turn it off entirely carefully.

It's worth keeping your iPhone 11 constant on the surface, or perhaps a tripod if you have one, as the telephone will recognize this and raise the shutter rate to 30 mere seconds, which is potentially ideal for night sky photos.

5. <u>Grasp the ultra-wide-angle lens</u>

The iPhone 11 and iPhone 11 Pro will be the first ones with a super wide-angle lens. If you haven't used one before, their 13mm equivalent field of view will come in super-handy for several different subjects, but particularly landscape and architecture, where you want to fit in as much of the scene as possible.

If you wish to exceed dramatic building pictures, one common technique utilized by professional scenery photographers is to juxtapose one close object with a distant object - for example, some close by plants with a long way background subject.

You could also want to use it in a while composing in portrait orientation, for a fascinating new look that wouldn't have been possible before with older iPhones.

6. *Portrait setting is not only for humans*

Even though iPhone XR had a great camera, you couldn't use the inbuilt Family portrait mode for anything apart from human subjects. Bad information for pet-lovers, or merely those who wish to create a shallow depth of field results with any subject.

That's all transformed for the iPhone 11, which uses its two digital cameras to help you to take shallow depth-of-field impact images for many different subjects, and has been specially optimised for domestic pets. To begin with, all you have to do is swipe to *Family portrait mode* and point the camera the four-legged friend. It'll tell you if you're too near to the subject and instruct you to move away. The details are nearly perfect, but they're perfect - particularly if you're looking on a little screen.

7. *Locate those lacking settings*

Through the keynote release of the iPhone 11 and iPhone 11 Pro, it was announced that the native camera application would be simplified to help you consider the key method of shooting your images.

That's great and produces a much cleaner interface, but it can imply that some configurations are now just a little concealed away. If you think where they've eliminated, touch the arrow near the top of the display, and you'll find a range of different alternatives, including aspect percentage (see below), adobe flash, night setting (if it's dark enough), timer and digital filter systems.

8. *Try the new 16:9 aspect ratio*

This is an attribute that is new for the iPhone 11 and

iPhone 11 Pro, adding a new aspect ratio to the prevailing 4:3 and square (1:1) options. Using a 16:9 aspect percentage is ways to get more full shots which ingest more of the scene, and also eventually screen very nicely on the iPhone display screen.

You'll need to activate it from the menu - the default is 4:3. It's well worth also using the 16:9 aspect proportion with the ultra-wide position to get some good great breathtaking type shots.

CHAPTER 10

Restoring iPhone 11 Backup from iCloud and iTunes

There is no need connecting your brand-new iPhone 11 Series (iPhone 11, iPhone 11 Pro, and iPhone 11 Pro Max) to your personal computer, as long as there is a mobile data connection designed for activation. As you end the set-up wizard, you may navigate back by tapping the back arrow at the top left-hand side of the screen and scroll further to another display by tapping another button at the top right-hand corner.

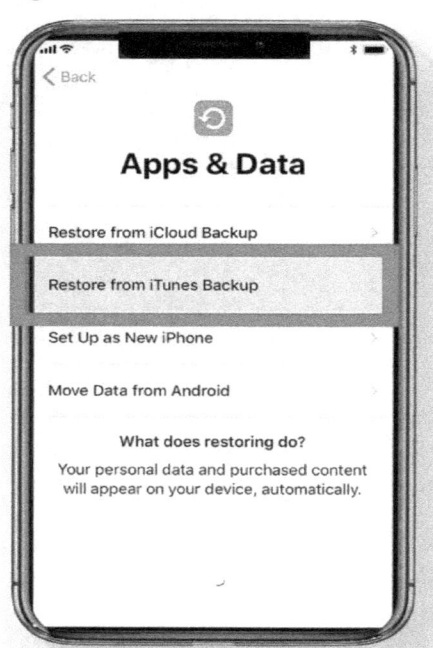

You can commence by pressing down the power button at the top edge of your brand-new iPhone 11 Series (iPhone 11, iPhone 11 Pro and iPhone 11 Pro Max). You may want to keep it pressed down for about two seconds until you notice a vibration, meaning the iPhone 11 Series (iPhone 11, iPhone 11 Pro and iPhone 11 Pro Max) is booting up.

Once it boots up finally, you can start initial set up by following the processes below;

- Swipe your finger over the display screen to start the set-up wizard.
- Choose the language of preference - English is usually at the top of the list, so there is no problem finding it. However, if you would like to apply a different language, scroll down to look for your desired *language,* and tap to select the preferred language.
- Choose your *country* - the *United States,* for instance, which may be close to the top of the list. If otherwise, scroll down the list and select the

United States or any of your choice.

- You need to connect your iPhone 11 Series (iPhone 11, iPhone 11 Pro, and iPhone 11 Pro Max) to the internet to start its activation. You can test this via a link with a Wi-Fi network. Locate the name of your available network in the list shown, and then tap on it to select it.

- Enter the Wi-Fi security password (you will generally find this written on your router, which is probably known as the WPA Key, WEP Key, or Password) and select Sign up. A tick indication shows you are connected, and a radio image appears near the top of the screen. The iPhone 11 Series (iPhone 11, iPhone 11 Pro, and iPhone 11 Pro Max) would now start activation with Apple automatically. It may take some time!

- In case your iPhone 11 Series (iPhone 11, iPhone 11 Pro, and iPhone 11 Pro Max) is a 4G version, you would be requested to check for updated internet configurations after inserting a new Sim card. You can test this anytime, so, for the present time, tap **Continue**.

- Location services would help you with mapping, weather applications, and more, giving you specific information centred wholly on what your location is. Select whether to use location service by tapping allow location services.
- You would now be requested to create **Touch ID,** which is Apple's fingerprint identification. **Touch ID** allows you to unlock your iPhone 11 Series (iPhone 11, iPhone 11 Pro, and iPhone 11 Pro Max) with your fingerprint instead of your passcode or security password. To set up Tap Identification, put a finger or your thumb on the home button (but do not press it down!). To by-pass this for the moment, tap *setup Touch ID later*.
- If you are establishing Touch ID, the tutorial instruction on the screen will walk you through the set-up process. Put your finger on the home button, then remove it till the iPhone 11 Series (iPhone 11, iPhone 11 Pro, and iPhone 11 Pro Max) has properly scanned your fingerprint. Whenever your print is wholly scanned, you would notice a screen letting you know that tap recognition is successful.

Tap **Continue**.

- You would be requested to enter a passcode to secure your iPhone 11 Series (iPhone 11, iPhone 11 Pro, and iPhone 11 Pro Max). If you create **Touch ID**, you must use a passcode if, in any case, your fingerprint isn't acknowledged. Securing your computer data is an excellent idea, and the iPhone 11 Series (iPhone 11, iPhone 11 Pro, and iPhone 11 Pro Max) provides you with several options. Tap password option to choose your lock method.

- You can arrange a Custom Alphanumeric Code (that is a security password that uses characters and figures), a Custom Numeric Code (digit mainly useful, however, you can add as many numbers as you want!) or a 4-Digit Numeric Code. In case you didn't install or set up **Touch ID,** you may even have an option not to add a Security password. Tap on your selected Security option.

- I would recommend establishing a 4-digit numeric code, or Touch ID for security reasons, but all optional setup is done likewise. Input your selected Security password using the keyboard.

- Verify your Security password by inputting it again. If the Password does not match, you'll be requested to repeat! If indeed they do match, you'll continue to another display automatically.

At this time of the set-up process, you'll be asked whether you have used an iPhone 11 Series (iPhone 11, iPhone 11 Pro and iPhone 11 Pro Max) before and probably upgrading it, you can restore all of your applications and information from an iCloud or iTunes backup by deciding on the best option. If this is your first iPhone 11 Series (iPhone 11, iPhone 11 Pro and iPhone 11 Pro Max), you would have to get it started as new, yet, in case you are moving from Android to an iPhone 11 Series (iPhone 11, iPhone 11 Pro and iPhone 11 Pro Max), you can transfer all your data by deciding and choosing the choice you want.

How to Move Data From an Android Phone

Apple has made it quite easy to move your data from a Google Android device to your new iPhone 11 Series (iPhone 11, iPhone 11 Pro and iPhone 11 Pro Max).

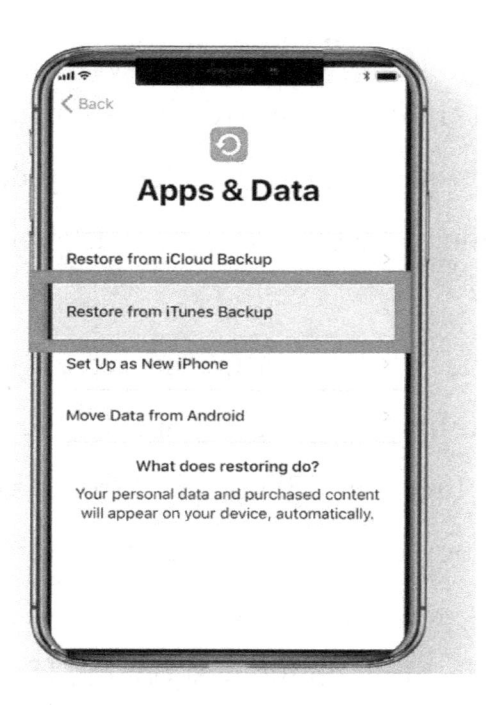

Proceed to the iOS app. I'll direct you about how to use the application to move your data!

- Using the iPhone 11 Series (iPhone 11, iPhone 11 Pro and iPhone 11 Pro Max), if you are on the applications & data screen of the set-up wizard, tap ***move data from Google android***.
- Go to the Play Store on your Google android device and download the app recommended by the set-up wizard. When it is installed, open up the app, select **Continue,** and you'll be shown the ***Terms & Conditions*** to continue.

- On your Android device, tap *Next* to start linking your Devices. On your own iPhone 11 Series (iPhone 11, iPhone 11 Pro, and iPhone 11 Pro Max), select ***Continue***.
- Your iPhone 11 Series (iPhone 11, iPhone 11 Pro, and iPhone 11 Pro Max) would show a 6-digit code that has to be received into the **Google android** device to set the two phones up.
- Your Google android device would screen all the data that'll be moved. By default, all options are ticked - so if there could be something you don't want to move, tap the related collection to deselect it. If you are prepared to continue, tap *Next* on your Google android device.
- As the change progresses, you would notice the iPhone 11 Series (iPhone 11, iPhone 11 Pro, and iPhone 11 Pro Max) display screen changes, showing you the position of the info transfer and progress report.
- When the transfer is completed, you will notice a confirmation screen on each device. On your Android Device, select ***Done*** to shut the app. On

your own iPhone 11 Series (iPhone 11, iPhone 11 Pro, and iPhone 11 Pro Max), tap *Continue*.

- An *Apple ID* allows you to download apps, supported by your iPhone 11 Series and synchronize data through multiple devices, which makes it an essential account you should have on your iPhone 11 Series! If you have been using an iPhone X phones previously, or use iTunes to download music to your laptop, then you should have already become an *Apple ID* user. Register with your username and passwords (when you have lost or forgotten your Apple ID or password, you will see a link that may help you reset it). If you're not used to iPhone 11 Series (iPhone 11, iPhone 11 Pro and iPhone 11 Pro Max), select doesn't have an Apple ID to create one for free.

- The Terms & Conditions for your iPhone 11 Series (iPhone 11, iPhone 11 Pro and iPhone 11 Pro Max) can be seen. Please go through them (tapping on more to study additional info), so when you are done, tap *Agree*.

- You'll be asked about synchronizing your data

with iCloud. That's to ensure bookmarks, connections, and other items of data are supported securely with your other iPhone 11 Series (iPhone 11, iPhone 11 Pro, and iPhone 11 Pro Max)'s data. Tap ***merge*** to permit this or ***don't merge*** if you'll have a choice to keep your details elsewhere asides iCloud.

- **Apple pay** is Apple's secure payment system that stores encrypted credit or debit card data on your device and making use of your iPhone 11 Series (iPhone 11, iPhone 11 Pro, and iPhone 11 Pro Max) also with your fingerprint to make safe transactions online and with other apps. Select *Next* to continue.

- To *feature/add a card*, place it on a set surface and place the iPhone 11 Series (iPhone 11, iPhone 11 Pro, and iPhone 11 Pro Max) over it, so the card is put in the camera framework. The credit card info would be scanned automatically, and you would be requested to verify that the details on display correspond with your card. You'll also be asked to enter the *CVV* (safety code) from the personal strip behind the card. If you choose (or the camera cannot recognize your cards), you can enter credit card information by hand by tapping the hyperlink. You could bypass establishing **Apple Pay** by tapping *create later*.

- Another screen discusses the *iCloud keychain*, which is Apple's secure approach to sharing your preserved security password and payment information throughout all your Apple devices. You might use *iCloud security code* to validate your brand-new device and import present data, or you might be asked to continue registering your keychain if it's your first Apple device. In case you don't want to share vital data with other devices, you should go to *avoid iCloud keychain* or *don't restore passwords*.

- If you want to set up your Apple keychain, you'd be notified to either use a Security password (the same one you'd set up on your iPhone 11 Series (iPhone 11, iPhone 11 Pro, and iPhone 11 Pro Max)) or produce a different code. If you're making use of your iCloud security code, you should put it on your iPhone 11 Series (iPhone 11, iPhone 11 Pro, and iPhone 11 Pro Max) when prompted.

- This would confirm your ID when signing on to an iCloud safety code; a confirmation code would be delivered via SMS. You may want to hyperlink your smartphone text code (if you have never distributed one with Apple already) so that the code may be provided as a text. Then enter this code to your iPhone 11 Series (iPhone 11, iPhone 11 Pro, and iPhone 11 Pro Max) if requested, then select *Next.*

- You'll then be asked to create **Siri**. *Siri* is your own digital personal associate, which might search the internet, send communications, and check out data in your device and a lot more, all without having to flick via specific apps. Choose to create Siri by tapping the choice or start Siri later to skip this task for now.

- To set up and create SIRI, you would need to speak several phrases to the iPhone 11 Series (iPhone 11, iPhone 11 Pro, and iPhone 11 Pro Max) to review your conversation patterns and identify your voice.

- Once you say every term, a tick would be observed, showing that it's been known and comprehended. Another phrase may indicate that you should read aloud.

- Once you've completed the five phrases, you would notice a display notifying that Siri has been set up correctly. Tap ***Continue***.

- The iPhone 11 Series (iPhone 11, iPhone 11 Pro, and iPhone 11 Pro Max) display alters the colour balance to help make the screen show up naturally under distinctive light conditions. You can switch this off in the screen settings after the iPhone 11 Series (iPhone 11, iPhone 11 Pro, and iPhone 11 Pro Max) has completed configuring it. Tap ***continue*** to continue with the setup.

- Has your iPhone 11 Series (iPhone 11, iPhone 11 Pro, and iPhone 11 Pro Max) been restored? Tap begin to transfer your computer data to your brand-new iPhone 11 Series (iPhone 11, iPhone 11 Pro, and iPhone 11 Pro Max).

- You'll be prompted to ensure your brand-new iPhone 11 Series (iPhone 11, iPhone 11 Pro and iPhone 11 Pro Max) has enough power to avoid the device turning off in the process of downloading applications and information. Tap *OK* to verify this recommendation.
- You would notice a notification show up on your apps to download in the background.

NB: Setting up any new iPhone model: A similar method, as described above, applies.

How to Restore iPhone 11 Back-up from iCloud or iTunes

If you want to restore your iPhone 11 Series (iPhone 11, iPhone 11 Pro, and iPhone 11 Pro Max) from an iTunes back-up, you may want to connect to iCloud and have the latest version of iTunes installed on it. If you are ready to begin this process, tap **restore** from iTunes back-up on your iPhone 11 Series and connect it to your personal computer. Instructions about how to bring back your data can be followed on the laptop screen.

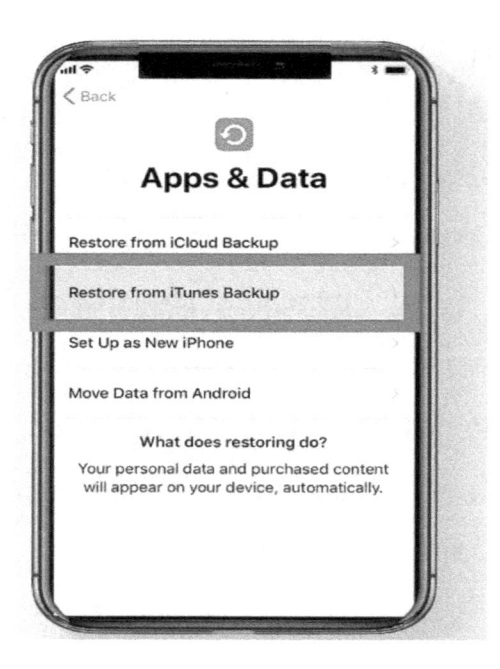

In case your old iPhone model was supported on iCloud, then follow the instructions below to restore your applications & data to your brand-new device:

- Tap **Restore** from iCloud back-up.
- Register with the Apple ID and Password that you applied to your old iPhone. If you fail to recollect the security password, there's a link that may help you reset it.
- The Terms & Conditions screen would show. Tap the links to learn about specific areas in detail. When you are ready to proceed, select **Agree**.

- Your iPhone 11 Series (iPhone 11, iPhone 11 Pro, and iPhone 11 Pro Max) would need some moments to create your Apple ID and hook up with the iCloud server.
- You would notice a summary of available backups to download. The most up-to-date backup would be observed at the very top, with almost every other option below it. If you want to restore from a desirable backup, tap the screen for ***all backups*** to see the available choices.
- Tap on the back-up you want to restore to start installing.
- A progress bar would be shown, providing you with a demo of the advancement of the download. When the restore is completed, the device will restart.
- You would see a notification telling you that your iPhone 11 Series (iPhone 11, iPhone 11 Pro, and iPhone 11 Pro Max) is updated effectively. Tap ***Continue***.
- To complete the iCloud set up on your recently restored iPhone 11 Series (iPhone 11, iPhone 11

Pro, and iPhone 11 Pro Max), you should re-enter your iCloud (Apple ID) password. Enter/review it and then tap *Next*.

- You'll be prompted to upgrade the security information related to your *Apple ID*. Tap on any stage to replace your computer data, or even to bypass this option. If you aren't ready to do this, then tap the *Next* button.

- **Apple pay** is Apple's secure payment system that stores encrypted credit or debit card data on your device and making use of your iPhone 11 Series (iPhone 11, iPhone 11 Pro, and iPhone 11 Pro Max) also with your fingerprint to make safe transactions online and with other apps. Select *Next* to continue.

- To *feature/add a card*, place it on a set surface and place the iPhone 11 Series (iPhone 11, iPhone 11 Pro, and iPhone 11 Pro Max) over it, so the card is put in the camera framework. The credit card info would be scanned automatically, and you would be requested to verify that the details on display correspond with your card. You'll also be asked to enter the *CVV* (safety code) from the personal strip behind the card. If you choose (or the camera cannot recognize your cards), you can enter credit card information by hand by tapping the hyperlink. You could bypass establishing **Apple Pay** by tapping *create later*.

- Another screen discusses the *iCloud keychain*, which is Apple's secure approach to sharing your preserved security password and payment information throughout all your Apple devices. You might use *iCloud security code* to validate your brand-new device and import present data, or you might be asked to continue registering your keychain if it's your first Apple device. In case you don't want to share vital data with other devices, you should go to *avoid iCloud keychain* or *don't restore passwords*.

- If you selected to set up your Apple keychain, you'd be notified to either uses a Security password (the same one you'd set up on your iPhone 11 Series (iPhone 11, iPhone 11 Pro and iPhone 11 Pro Max)) or provide a different code. If you're making use of your iCloud security code, you should put it on your iPhone 11 Series (iPhone 11, iPhone 11 Pro, and iPhone 11 Pro Max) when prompted.

- This would confirm your ID when signing on to an iCloud safety code; a confirmation code would be delivered via SMS. You may want to hyperlink your smartphone text code (if you have never distributed one with Apple already) so that the code may be provided as a text. Then enter this code to your iPhone 11 Series (iPhone 11, iPhone 11 Pro, and iPhone 11 Pro Max) if requested, then select *Next.*

- You'll then be asked to create **Siri**. *Siri* is your own digital personal associate, which might search the internet, send communications, and check out data in your device and a lot more, all without having to flick via specific apps. Choose to create Siri by tapping the choice or start Siri later to skip this task for now.

- To set up and create SIRI, you would need to speak several phrases to the iPhone 11 Series (iPhone 11, iPhone 11 Pro, and iPhone 11 Pro Max) to review your conversation patterns and identify your voice.

- Once you say every term, a tick would be observed, showing that it's been known and comprehended. Another phrase may indicate that you should read aloud.
- Once you've completed the five phrases, you would notice a display notifying that Siri has been set up correctly. Tap *Continue*.
- The iPhone 11 Series (iPhone 11, iPhone 11 Pro, and iPhone 11 Pro Max) display alters the colour balance to help make the screen show up naturally under distinctive light conditions. You can switch this off in the screen settings after the iPhone 11 Series (iPhone 11, iPhone 11 Pro, and iPhone 11 Pro Max) has completed configuring it. Tap *continue* to continue with the setup.
- Has your iPhone been restored? Tap begin to transfer your computer data to your brand-new iPhone 11 Series (iPhone 11, iPhone 11 Pro, and iPhone 11 Pro Max).

- You'll be prompted to ensure your brand-new iPhone 11 Series (iPhone 11, iPhone 11 Pro and iPhone 11 Pro Max) has enough charge to avoid the device turning off in the process of downloading applications and information. Tap *OK* to verify this recommendation.
- You would notice a notification show up on your apps to download in the background.

Chapter 11

How to start Dark Mode on iPhone 11

First, check out *'Configurations'* and then look for *'Screen & Lighting.'* Once there, you'll see an all-new interface that places dark setting front side and centre. You will toggle between *'Light'* and *'Dark'* mode with only a tap, assuming you want to activate it manually; however, its implementation within iOS is just a little smarter than either 'on' or 'off.'

Under the two main options, you'll also visit a toggle

marked *'Automatic'* which, as you may be able to think, switches dark setting on alone, linked with sunset and sunrise. Additionally, you then have the choice to define specific times for dark settings to allow and disable.

Dark mode has shown to be one of the very most hyped features approaching to cellular devices in 2019. It isn't just a capability destined for iOS 13 either, it's a significant feature in Google android ten plus some devices have previously instigated their own undertake dark setting - cell phones like the Asus ZenFone 6 and the OnePlus 7 Pro.

What does Dark Mode in iOS 13 do?

A part of dark mode's charm originates from the decrease in power usage it brings, particularly on devices that use OLED shows, like the iPhone X, XS, and XS Maximum. Beyond power intake, however, darker interface shades also lessen eye strain, particularly when being viewed in dark surroundings. In some cases, alternative UI and font colours are also associated with alleviating conditions like Scotopic Level of sensitivity Syndrome - an affliction commonly within people that have dyslexia, which makes text visibility and comprehension difficult.

How to Upgrade Applications on your iPhone in iOS 13

If you're used to manually updating your applications on either an iPhone, iPad or iPod touch by going to the updates tabs in the App Store, then iOS 13 has made some changes. That tabs has eliminated and has been changed by *Arcade*. If you don't anticipate using the new Apple Arcade membership video gaming service, then there's no chance to eliminate this.

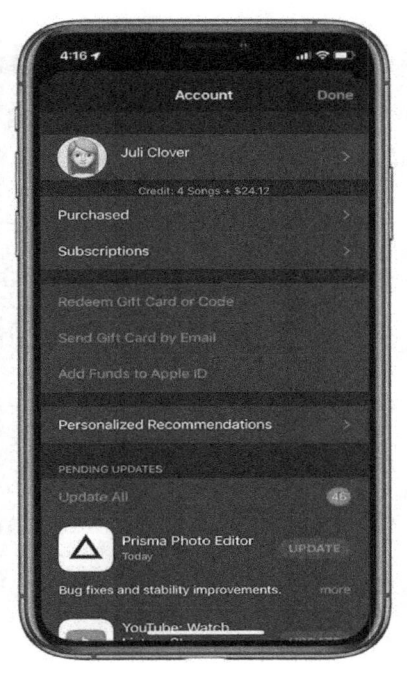

Here's how to revise your applications in iOS 13:

- Start the App Store on your iPhone.

- Tap the round consumer icon at the right-hand corner.

- Scroll down, and you'll see a list of all of your applications that either have updates available or have been recently updated.

- If an application comes with an update available, you can hit the button to start it manually.

Do applications automatically upgrade in iOS 13?

It appears clear that the reason behind Apple moving this program is because applications tend to update themselves quietly in the background, removing the necessity for anybody to manage application updates manually. The downside with this is that it could be challenging to learn what new features have found its way to applications if you're not looking at the release notes.

Chapter 12

iPhone 11 Tips & Tricks

Control Your Apple TV With iPhone 11

The Control Focus on the iPhone 11 has an impressive trick: it enables you to regulate your Apple TV if you have one. As long as your iPhone 11 and Apple Television are on a single cellular network, it'll work. Get into Control Centre and then look for the Apple Television button that shows up. Touch it and start managing your Apple Television.

How to Enable USB Restricted Setting on iPhone 11

Apple just built a robust new security feature into the iPhone 11 with the latest version of iOS; this launch is what's known as **USB Restricted Setting** to the iPhone 11. Lately, companies have been making devices that may be connected to an iPhone's USB slot and crack an iPhone's passcode.

To protect from this, Apple has introduced a USB Restricted Setting. USB Restricted Setting disabled data writing between an iPhone and a USB device if the iPhone is not unlocked to get more than one hour; this effectively makes the iPhone breaking boxes ineffective as they may take hours or times to unlock a locked iPhone.

By default, **USB Restricted Mode** is enabled in iOS. But for those who want to disable it, or make sure it hasn't been disabled, go to the *Configurations app* and touch *Face ID & Passcode*. Enter your passcode and then swipe down until you visit a section entitled ***"Allow Access When Locked."***

The final toggle in this section is a field that says *"USB Accessories."* The toggle next to them should be turned OFF (white); this implies *USB Restricted Setting* is allowed, and devices can't download or upload data from/to your iPhone if the iPhone is not unlocked to get more than one hour.

Use Two Pane Scenery View

This tip only pertains to the iPhone 11 Pro Max but is cool nonetheless. If you keep your XS device horizontally when using specific applications, you'll see lots of the built-in apps changes to a two-pane setting, including Email and Records. This setting is the main one you observe on an iPad where, for example, you can see a list of all of your records in the Records app while positively reading or editing a single note.

How to stop iPhone 11 Alarms with Your Face

An extremely cool feature of the iPhone 11 is Face ID. It gives you to unlock your phone just by taking a look at it. Face ID also has various other cool features-like that one. Whenever your iPhone 11 or XS security alarm goes off, you could silent it by just picking right up your iPhone and taking a look at it; this tells your iPhone you understand about the arm, and it'll quiet it.

Quickly Disable Face ID

Depending on your geographical area, the police might be able to legally demand you uncover your smartphone at that moment via its facial recognition features. For reasons unknown, facial biometrics aren't protected in the manner fingerprints, and passcodes are; in a few localities. That's why Apple has generated an attribute that lets you quickly disable Face ID in a pinch without going into your settings. Just press the side button five times, and Face ID will be disabled, and you'll need to enter your passcode instead to gain access to your phone.

How to slow the two times click necessary for Apple Pay

Given that the iPhone 11 jettisoned the Touch ID sensor, you confirm your *Apple Pay* obligations by using Face ID and twice pressing the medial side button. By default, you would need to dual press the medial side button pretty quickly-but it is possible to make things slow down.

To take action, go to *Settings > General > Availability*. Now scroll right down to Side Button. Privately Button screen, you can select between *default, gradual, or slowest*. Pick the speed that is most effective for you.

Chapter 13

How to Maximize iPhone 11

Gestures on the iPhone's touchscreen will always be necessary, but without the Home button, the iPhone 11, and later models, gestures become essential. To execute functions just like a turnoff or time for the Home screen on your iPhone 11, 11 Pro and 11 Pro Max, you are going to use unique gestures that combine the medial side and Volume control keys instead of the lacking Home button.

Common features, like speaking with Siri, starting **Apple Pay**, and shutting apps, will have unique gestures that Utilize your phone's physical control keys, Face ID, and the touchscreen. This chapter addresses all the tips you should know, like how to use Reachability, have a screenshot, as well as how to briefly disable Face ID the iPhone 11, 11 Pro and 11 Pro Max. Let's get started doing how to use gestures to get around iPhone models X and later.

There are a significant number of new gestures and changes to navigate the iPhone, given that Apple did away with the Home button. You're probably acquainted with the most common iPhone gestures, such as pinching with two fingertips to focus or Tremble to Undo. You can also pull multiple photos and drop them into another app. Gestures on the iPhone would always be an integral part of the routine. However, the iPhone 11 launched a lot of new ways to do old stuff. Unless in any other case, indicated these procedures all connect with the iPhone 11, 11 Pro, and 11 Pro Max.

How to Unlock Your iPhone with Raise to Wake

Raise to Wake is fired up by default on the iPhone 11 and other newer models. To use *Raise to Wake* on the iPhone 11, 11 Pro and 11 Pro Max, lift your iPhone, and the screen would automatically start. If *Raise to Wake* isn't working, likely, you have accidentally handicapped the feature inside Configurations.

How to Enable Raise to Wake:

- Open up the *Settings* app.

- Select *Screen & Brightness*.

- Toggle Raise to Wake to the ON position to allow the feature.

You don't need to lift your phone awaken the screen on iPhone 11; you can merely touch the screen to awaken your iPhone 11, even if Raise to Wake is impaired.

How to Unlock the iPhone 11 & Newer iPhones

To unlock your iPhone 11, 11 Pro and 11 Pro Max, or 11, you would need to ensure that a Face ID is established. Using Face ID, you can boost or tap your iPhone 11, or other newer models, to wake and unlock your iPhone by looking straight at the screen.

How exactly to Unlock an iPhone 11 or Later Using Face ID:

- Wake the screen up by either tapping the screen or using Raise to Wake.

- Look directly at the screen to use Face ID to unlock your device.

- Swipe up from underneath of your Lock screen to visit the Home screen.

- If, for just about any reason, Face ID didn't unlock your mobile phone, swipe up from underneath of the screen to retry Face ID or even to enter your passcode instead. Once you have input your passcode, your iPhone will automatically go back to the Home screen, or whatever application was open up last.

How to Open up the Control & Notification Centres

The notch on the iPhone 11 and later models divide the very best of the screen into a left and right hands screen. On your own iPhone 11, 11 Pro and 11 Pro Max, the right part of the notch near the top of the screen is used to gain access to your Control Centre while the left side is utilized to open up Notifications.

- To open Control Centre, swipe down from the right-hand side of the screen.

- To open Notifications, swipe down from the left-hand side of the screen.

How to Go back to the Home screen From an App

Returning to the home screen can appear impossible if there is no Home button. Around the iPhone 11, 11 Pro and 11 Pro Max, and 11, you can go back to your home screen by following the instructions below.

How to Go back to the Home Screen:

- From within any app, place your finger on the home bar underneath the center of the screen.

- Swipe up toward the very top of your screen.

How to Activate Apple Pay

On previous iPhone models, twice tapping the home button raised Apple Pay from a locked screen, but on the iPhone 11 or later, you will have to use a new gesture to gain access to **Apple Pay**. To use Apple Pay from a locked screen on the iPhone 11, 11 Pro and 11 Pro Max, you will have to double click your side button and use Face ID to continue with Apple Pay. Here's how to use

Apple Pay on iPhones without a Home button:

- Double click on the Part button to open up Apple Pay

- Look into your iPhone screen to verify with Face ID.

If Apple Pay doesn't appear when the medial side button is double-clicked, 1 of 2 things is undoubtedly going on: either you haven't created a debit card with Apple Pay (check even though you have; my cards disappeared after establishing my new iPhone) or you do not have Apple Pay allowed in settings; this is fixed with the next steps:

- Open up the Settings app.

- Select Face ID & Passcode.

- Toggle ON **Apple Pay** under Use **Face ID** For.

How to Power Off the iPhone 11

Sometimes, you will need to power your iPhone off for a movie, a lecture, or other events that want your full attention. Like previous models, whenever your iPhone 11, 11 Pro and 11 Pro Max, are a runoff, then you will have to use a gesture to turn your iPhone back On carefully.

To carefully *Turn On* the iPhone 11 or later models, press and maintain the side button before the Apple logo design appears.

How to Access Siri with Side Button

Removing the home button also changes how you access Siri on the iPhone 11 and newer models.

- If you wish to use gestures rather than Hey Siri on the iPhone 11, 11 Pro and 11 Pro Max, then you will have to use the medial side button to gain access to Siri.

- Click and hold the Side button (formerly known as the Rest/Wake button) to speak to Siri.

How to Take Screenshots without the home Button

Sometimes, you would need to have a screenshot to save lots of a great formula as a graphic or to keep hold of a text to examine later.

- To have a screenshot on the iPhone 11, 11 Pro and 11 Pro Max, you'll use a mixture of the medial side and volume buttons rather than utilizing a Home button.

- To consider screenshot on your iPhone 11, or a later model iPhone, concurrently press and release the medial side button and Volume Up button.

How to Enable & Activate Reachability

Reachability slashes off the low fifty percent of the screen and moves the very best part of your screen to underneath, making it simpler to reach the very best of your display with one hand. By default, Reachability has switched off on the iPhone X, XS, XS Max, and iPhone 11 Series phone; nevertheless, you can allow the Reachability feature inside the Settings portion of your Configurations app.

To allow Reachability on your iPhone 11, 11 Pro, and 11 Pro Max:

- Open up the *Settings* app.

- Select *General*.

- Touch *Accessibility*.

- Toggle on *Reachability*.

- Swipe down on the home bar or bottom level middle of the screen to activate Reachability.

Given that you've allowed Reachability, you can enable the feature within any application by swiping down on the horizontal part, also called the home feature, at the bottom of your screen. There is no home pub on the home screen; nevertheless, you can still activate Reachability on the home screen by swiping down from underneath the middle of the screen where you'll typically find the home feature.

How to Change Between & Force Quit Apps

You would find two various ways to change between applications on the iPhone 11: with the App Switcher and without. You can gain access to the App Switcher on the iPhone 11, 11 Pro and 11 Pro Max, by partly swiping upwards from underneath the screen. You can even switch between applications by swiping the home bar still left or right.

How to Open up the App Switcher on the iPhone

- Swipe halfway up from underneath the screen.

- Lift your finger, and the App Switcher would open up. You can swipe through, much like previous models, and touch on an application to open up it.

- To eliminate an application from App Switcher, swipe through to the app.

To switch applications without starting the App Switcher:

- Place your finger on the home bar or underneath the middle of the screen if the home button is absent.

- Swipe from left to open up your latest applications in descending order.

How to Switch OFF Power & Perform a Hard Restart

The Home button was central to numerous functions, including powering down your iPhone or forcing a hard restart whenever your iPhone freeze. To shut down or push a hard reset on the iPhone 11, 11 Pro, and 11 Pro Max, you would have to perform new gestures that involve a mixture of the medial side and Volume Up buttons.

To turn from the iPhone 11, 11 Pro and 11 Pro Max:

- Hold down the medial side button and the Volume Up or Down button before the option to slip to power off shows up.

- Using the Slip to Force Off toggle, swipe to the right.

You can even switch off the iPhone 11, iPhone 11 Pro, and iPhone 11 Pro Max from the overall portion of the Settings app.

- Open up the Settings application and choose *General*.

- Scroll entirely down to underneath, and tap TURN OFF.

- Glide to power icon to turn the power off.

You are capable of doing a hard restart, sometimes called a force shutdown, on your iPhone 11, iPhone 11 Pro, and iPhone 11 Pro Max. To execute a hard reboot:

- Quickly press and release the Volume Up accompanied by the Volume Down button.

- Now, press and maintain the side button before the device shuts down, and the Apple logo design appears.

- Your iPhone would automatically restart.

It's good to notice that whenever performing a hard Restart, it requires the iPhone 11 a couple of seconds to turn off when you're pressing the medial side button. So don't quit! I thought it wasn't working initially, but I needed to sustain the side button pressed down for a longer length of time.

How to Temporarily Disable Face ID

Face ID is not a perfect system; users have reported that some family members have had the opportunity to use cell phones protected Face ID due to a strong family resemblance. To briefly disable Face ID, you would have to keep down the medial side and Volume Up control keys to talk about the turn off-screen, and then tap Cancel to Force your iPhone to require the passcode to unlock briefly.

Here's how to briefly disable *Face ID* on the iPhone 11, 11 Pro and 11 Pro Max:

- Hold down the Volume Up or Down button and the medial side button simultaneously.

- After the shutdown screen appears, forget about the buttons. That is important; if you keep up to carry down the control keys, Emergency SOS would automatically be brought on.

- Touch the X at the bottom to cancel the shutdown.

Now, Face ID is briefly handicapped until you enter your passcode. Once you enter your passcode, Face ID would continue working as typical.

INDEX

1

1Password, **84**

3

3D, **14**, **34**, **38**, **77**, **97**, **109**

A

A12 chip, **34**

A13 Bionic CPU, **31**

activation, **122**, **124**

Alarm, **11**, **52**

Android, **127**, **129**

Animoji, **99**, **100**

Apple, **9**, **10**, **11**, **13**, **15**, **17**, **20**, **21**, **25**, **26**, **27**, **28**, **29**, **30**, **31**, **32**, **33**, **34**, **35**, **38**, **39**, **40**, **41**, **44**, **46**, **98**, **105**, **112**, **113**, **124**, **125**, **127**, **130**, **131**, **132**, **133**, **136**, **137**, **138**, **139**, **140**, **145**, **146**, **147**, **148**, **150**, **153**, **157**, **158**, **159**, **165**

Apple pay, **131**, **138**

Apple Watch, **112**

apps, **30**, **44**, **47**, **52**, **79**, **83**, **86**, **97**, **102**, **112**, **130**, **131**, **133**, **135**, **138**, **140**, **142**, **149**, **153**

Arcade, **145**

Atmos, **29**, **38**

Audio, **36**

Auto-Lock, **22**

B

backdrop, **18**

Background, **18**

Back-up, **13**, **20**, **135**

Battery, **111**

Bluetooth, **23**, **105**

brightness, **31**, **105**

Browser, **19**, **20**, **45**

C

Calendars, **17**, **18**, **21**

Camera, **26**, **29**, **30**, **35**, **36**, **37**, **38**, **106**, **116**, **117**

charger, **41**, **113**

Configurations, **10**, **13**, **14**, **15**, **16**, **18**, **19**, **20**, **21**, **22**, **23**, **24**, **44**, **49**, **50**, **101**, **103**, **104**, **110**, **111**, **112**, **143**, **148**, **154**, **161**

Control Centre, **10**, **44**, **97**, **103**, **104**, **105**, **106**, **111**, **112**, **147**, **156**

CREDIT CARDS, **19**

CVV, **131**, **139**

D

dark mode, **144**

Data, **127**

Design, **26**, **34**

digital cameras, **115**, **119**

Display Screen, **28**

DO NOT Disturb, **10**, **11**

Dolby, **29**, **38**

E

Email, **15**, **16**, **17**, **21**, **79**, **149**

Euclidean Lands, 91

F

f/2.4 aperture, **35**

Face ID, **13**, **14**, **37**, **50**, **52**, **84**, **110**, **148**, **149**, **150**, **153**, **155**, **157**, **158**, **165**, **166**

Face Identification, **9**, **33**, **37**

FaceTime, **99**

fingerprint, **33**, **125**, **126**, **131**, **138**

flash, **36**, **94**, **105**, **120**

Focos, **88**, **89**

Focus, **48**, **110**, **147**

Folders, **47**

frame, **37**, **115**

G

gestures, **46**, **96**, **152**, **153**, **159**, **163**

Giphy World, 92

GPU, **35**

GTD, **81**

H

Haptics, **43**, **44**

HDR, **106**, **117**

HEIF, **116**

Home, **46**, **48**, **74**, **75**, **76**, **77**, **97**, **112**, **152**, **153**, **155**, **156**, **157**, **158**, **160**, **163**

I

iCloud, **13**, **16**, **17**, **19**, **20**, **21**, **22**, **122**, **127**, **131**, **132**, **133**, **135**, **136**, **137**, **139**, **140**

iMessage, **23**

Instagram, **115**

iOS 13, **11**, **20**, **26**, **41**, **84**, **100**, **101**, **109**, **111**, **144**, **145**, **146**

iPhone 11, **9**, **10**, **11**, **12**, **14**, **25**, **26**, **27**, **28**, **29**, **30**, **31**, **32**, **33**, **34**, **35**, **36**, **38**, **39**, **40**, **41**, **46**, **74**, **79**, **80**, **81**, **82**, **83**, **84**, **85**, **86**, **87**, **88**, **90**, **91**, **92**, **96**, **100**, **103**, **106**, **107**, **109**, **110**, **111**, **113**, **114**, **115**, **116**, **117**, **118**, **119**, **120**, **122**, **123**, **124**, **125**, **126**, **127**, **128**, **129**, **130**, **131**, **132**, **133**, **134**, **135**, **137**, **138**, **139**, **140**, **141**, **142**, **147**, **149**, **150**, **152**, **153**, **154**, **155**, **156**, **157**, **158**, **159**, **160**, **161**, **162**, **163**, **164**, **165**

iPhone 11 Pro, **25**, **26**, **27**, **28**, **29**, **30**, **32**, **33**, **113**, **114**, **115**, **116**, **117**, **118**, **120**, **121**, **122**, **123**, **124**, **125**, **126**, **127**, **128**, **129**, **130**, **131**, **132**, **133**, **134**, **135**, **137**, **138**, **139**, **140**, **141**, **142**, **149**, **164**

iPhone 11 Pro max, **30**

iPhone 11 Pro Max, **33**, **122**, **123**, **124**, **125**, **126**, **127**, **128**, **129**, **130**, **131**, **132**, **133**, **134**, **135**, **137**, **138**, **139**, **140**, **141**, **142**, **149**, **164**

iPhone X, **10**, **130**, **144**, **161**

iPhone XR, **25**, **28**, **29**, **35**, **38**, **39**, **40**, **41**, **119**

iPhone XS, **25**, **32**

iTunes, **21**, **22**, **103**, **122**, **127**, **130**, **135**

K

keyboard, **45**, **109**, **126**

Keychain, **19**, **20**

L

Library, **21**

LTE, **41**

169

M

Mac PC, **23**, **29**

Macintosh, **19**

Memoji, **99**, **100**

Merge, 107

Music, **21**, **22**, **23**, **105**

N

Night mode, 118

Nighttime Sky, 93

notifications, **10**, **11**, **50**, **51**, **52**, **85**, **96**, **100**, **101**

O

OLED, **29**, **88**, **144**

OmniCentre, 81

P

password, **14**, **84**, **124**, **125**, **126**, **127**, **130**, **132**, **136**, **138**, **139**

Phone, **11**, **43**, **46**, **127**

Photos, **20**, **21**, **43**, **88**, **90**, **105**, **106**, **107**, **108**, **116**

pixel, **39**, **90**

portrait mode, **38**, **107**, **119**, **120**

Portrait Setting, **38**, **88**, **106**

Preferences, **23**

Q

Qi, **113**

QuickTake, **37**

R

Rest/Wake, **159**

restore, **127**, **132**, **135**, **136**, **137**, **139**

Retina, **29**

Ringtones, **42**, **43**

S

screen, **11**, **22**, **28**, **29**, **40**, **43**, **46**, **47**, **48**, **49**, **51**, **52**, **74**, **75**, **76**, **77**, **78**, **87**, **96**, **97**, **98**, **100**, **101**, **104**, **105**, **107**, **108**, **109**, **110**, **111**, **113**, **120**, **121**, **122**, **123**, **124**, **125**, **128**, **129**, **132**, **134**, **135**, **136**, **137**, **139**, **141**, **151**, **152**, **154**, **155**, **156**, **157**, **158**, **160**, **161**, **162**, **163**, **165**, **166**

selfie, **27**, **100**

sensor, **35**, **37**, **150**

Setup, **9**, **11**, **13**

shortcuts, **46**, **75**, **76**, **77**, **103**

shutter button, **39**

shutter speed, **118**

Siri, **45**, **50**, **77**, **98**, **103**, **133**, **134**, **140**, **141**, **153**, **159**

Slo-mo, **38**

Smartphone, **35**, **40**

SMS, **133**, **140**

Snapchat, **92**

speaker, **23**

T

Touch ID, **9**, **13**, **14**, **50**, **125**, **126**, **150**

TrueDepth, **37**

Twitterific, **85**, **86**

Two Pane Scenery View, **149**

U

U1 Chip, **39**

Undo, **153**

USB Limited Setting, **147**

USB Restricted Mode, **148**

USB Restricted Setting, **148**

V

Volume, **22**, **52**, **77**, **152**, **160**, **163**, **164**, **165**, **166**

W

Wallet, **20**

Wallpaper, **46**, **47**, **49**

Water-Resistance, **40**

Widgets, **52**

wireless, **33**

X

XDR, **29**

Z

Zoom, **36**

zoom lens, **36**, **89**, **114**, **115**, **116**

CPSIA information can be obtained
at www.ICGtesting.com
Printed in the USA
BVHW042104050122
625580BV00013B/591